Wilfred Powell

Wanderings in a wild country

Three years amongst the cannibals of New Britain

Wilfred Powell

Wanderings in a wild country
Three years amongst the cannibals of New Britain

ISBN/EAN: 9783337196417

Printed in Europe, USA, Canada, Australia, Japan

Cover: Foto ©Andreas Hilbeck / pixelio.de

More available books at **www.hansebooks.com**

TOBERRAN HOUSE, NEW IRELAND.   *Frontispiece.*

WANDERINGS

IN

A WILD COUNTRY;

OR,

THREE YEARS AMONGST THE CANNIBALS OF NEW BRITAIN.

BY

WILFRED POWELL, F.R.G.S., &c.

WITH MANY ILLUSTRATIONS FROM SKETCHES BY THE AUTHOR.
DRAWN BY J. MEDLAND, ESQ.

LONDON:
SAMPSON LOW, MARSTON, SEARLE, & RIVINGTON,
CROWN BUILDINGS, 188 FLEET STREET.
1883.

LONDON:
PRINTED BY WILLIAM CLOWES AND SONS, LIMITED,
STAMFORD STREET AND CHARING CROSS.

TO THE READER.

In the following pages I have tried to place before
you an account of the little known Islands of New
Britain and Duke of York as they really are,
especially describing the habits and manners of their
inhabitants; and if my style of doing this should
appear to be somewhat crude, I must ask you to
extend your indulgence to one who is more accustomed to handle the tiller than the pen, and to
writing his log than manuscript for the publisher.

However, I have been persuaded by those who
have a far greater knowledge of the literary world
than myself to publish what little I know of these
hitherto comparatively unknown parts; and should
it be found that I have been mistaken as to some of
my statements, then let me again beg your indulgence
and remind you that a lifetime would hardly suffice
to enable one to become so thoroughly acquainted
with these primitive races as to be able to write about
them without some hesitation. Indeed, the more
one sees of these most interesting people so much

the more does one become aware of the difficulties of obtaining authentic information of many of their customs.

I conclude with the hope that the following pages may be of use to many and interesting to all my readers.

Yours, &c.,

WILFRED POWELL.

CONTENTS.

CHAPTER I.

CHAPTER II.

CHAPTER III.

CHAPTER IV.

CHAPTER VIII.

CHAPTER IX.

APPENDIX.

LIST OF ILLUSTRATIONS.

LIST OF ILLUSTRATIONS.

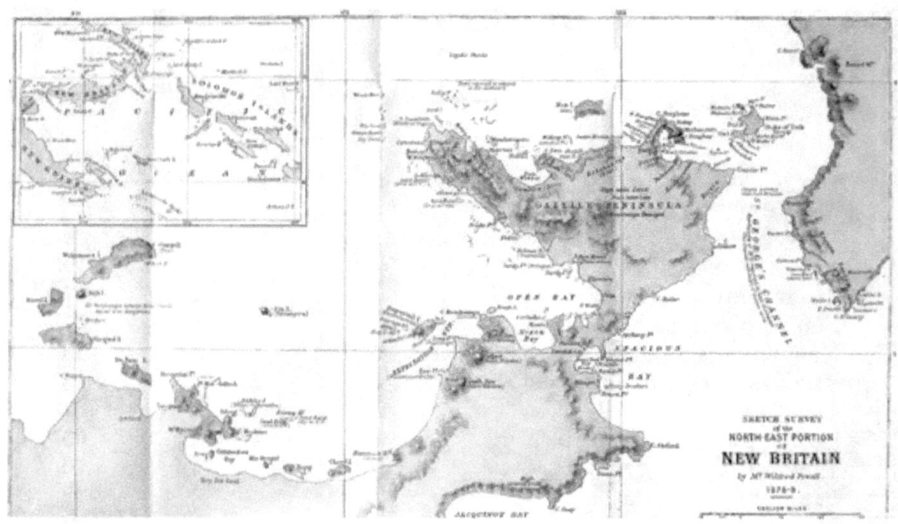

SKETCH SURVEY
of the
NORTH-EAST PORTION
of
NEW BRITAIN
by Mr Wilfred Powell
1878-9.
GAZELLE PENINSULA
ST GEORGE'S CHANNEL
OPEN BAY
SPACIOUS BAY
JACQUINOT BAY
SOLOMON ISLANDS

WANDERINGS IN A WILD COUNTRY;

OR,

THREE YEARS AMONGST THE CANNIBALS OF NEW BRITAIN.

CHAPTER I.

My vessel and crew—Encounter rough weather—Waterspouts—Courtesy of Captain Heath—Tragedy at Lizard Island—Brumer Islands—Teste Islands—Our cook and duck—Fighting implements and ornaments of natives of Heath Island—Women traders—Buying a petticoat—Possession Bay—Grandeur of the Pacific Islands—Natives of Hayter Island.

WITH the kind assistance of several gentlemen in Sydney, who were anxious to obtain information of the hitherto unknown parts of the Islands of New Britain and New Ireland, I purchased a small vessel of fifteen tons, which I considered would be amply large enough for safety among the numerous reefs and dangers we were likely to encounter. My experience has shown me that, among these islands, there are many and dangerous currents, which will place a vessel in danger of drifting on shore should it fall a calm; in this case a large vessel becomes perfectly helpless, but so small a craft as the one I obtained could be managed with sweeps, and by this means be kept off many dangers on to which a larger vessel must inevitably drift. Besides, a large vessel must keep a good distance from any island, which was just what we did not wish to do. Further, we could carry a small crew, therefore fewer men to grumble at any hardships we might have to put up with; and lastly, but certainly not of least consequence, we could get into places that no larger

"STAR OF THE EAST."

vessel could possibly attempt; moreover, it is useful at times to be able to run a vessel on to the lee-side of a reef or sandbank, should any repairs be necessary or the copper require cleaning.

Our little ketch, the *Star of the East*, having been docked, recoppered, and passed through the carpenters' hands, we stored her with all the necessities for a two years' voyage, and having fitted her as comfortably as was possible for so small a craft, we sailed on the 1st of June, 1877, from Sydney Heads.

I must now, before going any further, introduce the ship's company to the reader : myself the captain ; first lieutenant, H——— ; second, Jack ; third, Aleck (native of New Britain), and the cook (an American "darkie ") ; Rover, Bluff, and Pincher (better known as the "policemen "). A very fine crew, and very orderly, only one sailor having to be put on the black list before starting ; this was Rover, who would break out of the ship the moment I left the vessel, wishing to come after me, and therefore had to be tied up until we sailed, his attendance on shore not being required at that time, although of the utmost value afterwards.

We had a fine boat on deck, and a "stewardess" galley in a small corrugated iron house ; two bunks in the cabin, and a table ; two bunks in the forecastle, and two in the hold, the latter to be used in case of having any natives on board ; the crew slept under the boat on deck.

The first few days out we had calm weather, and made very little progress ; then came a strong breeze from the southward, and we proceeded some way on our journey. Off Port Stephens the wind increased to a gale, and blew very hard, veering round to the N.W. There was nothing for it but to heave to and wait till it moderated. That was a very anxious

time, as it blew a perfect hurricane, and our little
cockle-shell of a boat pitched and tossed as though
she were possessed, yet behaving splendidly, never
shipping a single sea, though the spray was blown
in sheets over the deck. The only trouble we had
was with the pump; the carpenters had left a
quantity of shavings under the skin, when replacing
it, and these were washed by the water she made
into the pump well and choked it. Of course it
would have been impossible for so small a vessel to
avoid making some water in so heavy a gale, and
besides this, we found that the deck was not as
watertight as it ought to have been. We had to
take the pump out, and in such heavy weather this
was no small matter; however, we managed it
successfully, cleared the shavings away and put
everything right again ; we lay hove to for four
days and nights.

On the third day a large barque came running
past with lower topsails and forecourse set ; she
hailed us to know if we wanted help—they could not
understand so small a craft being out such a long
distance from the land.

We observed a somewhat rare phenomenon (for
the latitude we were in) during this gale ; two
waterspouts passed at about half-a-mile from us,
working against the wind, and we distinctly heard
the rushing sound made by them above the noise of
the storm.

During the four days we lay hove to, we drifted
to windward, or " head reached," as sailors say, a

hundred and forty miles, but when again able to make sail, shaped our course for, and shortly afterwards anchored in, Trial Bay; then laying in a stock of fresh meat, bread, &c., we started again, with a fair wind, for Brisbane, reaching that port in a few days. With great courtesy, Captain Heath, R.N., Harbour Master, allowed us to lay alongside the Government wharf, where we took in water, had a square sail-yard fitted, laid in a necessary supply of onions, potatoes, &c., and obtained permission from the Government to enter all harbours on the Queensland coast free of dues. This shows the difference between the Governments of Queensland and New South Wales, for the latter, when asked for permission to ship bonded stores for our vessel, which was under fifty tons, and on a scientific survey, returned the polite (?) answer, " No departure from the law to be permitted."

From Brisbane we passed on to Townsville, sailing inside that wonderful " Great Barrier Reef," the terror of those that do not know it, the comfort of those that do. Leaving there we proceeded north, past Cooktown, and stood over to Lizard Island for firewood. This island was lately the scene of so sad a tragedy that I cannot refrain from giving the outlines of it here.

A Captain Watson formed a station on the island for fishing and curing " bêche-de-mer," where, with his wife, young child, and a number of Chinamen, he lived for some months. Having occasion to go to Cooktown in his schooner, he left his wife and child behind at the station, with a few of the Chinamen. He had not been gone long before a number of blacks from the mainland landed and attacked the station and the inmates, murdering some of the Chinamen and *eating* them; but Mrs. Watson, with *one* Chinaman, made such a resolute defence from the house (so it appears from the account in her diary written at the time) that the blacks were driven off for a period.

Fearing their return, Mrs. Watson and the Chinaman took one of the vessels that had been used for boiling the bêche-de-mer (a large iron tank cut in half), and somehow managed to rig up a mast in it; in this unwieldly craft Mrs. Watson, her baby, and the Chinaman started for another island some twenty miles off, under cover of the night, to escape observation by the blacks. They reached the island in safety, but seeing native canoes during the day, they again started for another island, thirty miles distant from their first refuge, but on neither of the islands did they find any water, and had none with them. In the meantime Captain Watson had returned to find his home and station sacked, and no traces of the missing ones, except a few articles of his wife's clothing, some of her hair, and the bones of the Chinamen that the blacks had eaten. He captured one of the black women, who described to him in the most graphic manner the murder of his wife and child; how Mrs. Watson had eventually been tomahawked and the body thrown into the water—she even pointed out the spot; but when divers were sent down nothing of course was found—this at the time was attributed to the sharks; she also said that the baby had been kept for a time, but because it would not stop crying one of the natives dashed its brains out. Her story was such a well-connected lie that it was believed by the unhappy man, and vengeance was accordingly taken on the supposed murderers.

Some time after a Captain Bremner, having occasion to call at the island on which Mrs. Watson had last taken refuge, discovered the bodies, and what confirmed their identity beyond all doubt was Mrs. Watson's diary, which he found near her body, written apparently up to a short time before her death, which was caused from want of water. It appears they saw a steamer pass and tried to attract attention, but failed. Mrs. Watson's last entry was to this effect, " Chinaman gone away to die by himself in the bush; baby very fretful and weak." No word of her own sufferings; not once is there to be found any complaint for herself entered in the whole of her diary, which was written in a firm, bold hand. What a noble spirit passed away in silent anguish on that lonely island! One of the search parties looking for traces actually landed on that very island, but *did not go on the right side of it.*

After taking in wood and water at Lizard Island, we shaped a course for the Barrier Reef, and passed out through the same passage by which Captain Cook passed in on board the *Endeavour* in 1770. We had a splendid strong fair wind, which soon carried us past and clear of the "Osprey Reef" in a N.W. course, and in a few days we sighted Brumer Islands. These islands are high and rocky, the highest peak being six hundred and sixty-five feet, according to the latest Admiralty chart. Here we found discoloured water where the Admiralty chart gives "twenty fathoms and no bottom;" this, however, has probably risen since the soundings marked on the Admiralty chart were taken. This shoal lies to the N.E. of the largest island.

I am sorry to say I was too busy at the time to take any soundings or cross-bearings, but the shoal is of large extent and easily observed from the masthead. I should say there were about three fathoms in the shallowest place we passed over. Several canoes came off, the natives appeared friendly and wished to trade. We bought a few little articles they had in the canoes, but being anxious to get on to Teste Island did not stop long.

The natives of the Brumer Islands are a dark race of the same type as those of the Gulf of Papua, but somewhat darker than the natives of China Straits and surrounding islands.

The following day we reached Teste Island, and anchored on the north side, about three hundred yards from the shore, as the water is too deep further off. The natives were very friendly, and brought off cocoa-nuts, yams, fish, and other articles, which they exchanged for iron hoop, red cloth, and beads.

We went on shore to visit the village, which lies on the south side of the island, there being only a

few huts on the north side. The houses are built on
piles from four to six feet high; on these are placed
large round pieces of wood, and on these rests the
house. These large plates of wood are for keeping off
snakes, rats, &c. The house seems to consist of roof
and floor only, for the roof is rounded off to each
side, something like an inverted boat; it is thatched
with grass or sugar-cane leaves; the floor is made of

NATIVE HOUSE, TESTE ISLAND, NEW GUINEA.

canes laid across the beams, and lashed together with
plaited string made of cocoa-nut fibre. The door is
only an opening on one side, approached by a rude
ladder constructed of forked stakes with pieces of
wood laid across in the forks. Inside the house
there is not room enough for a man to stand upright.
They sometimes make a small fire on a large flat
stone in the centre of the house, but most of the

cooking is done outside. The framework of the roof is made from bamboo cane, and the interior of almost every house was blackened by the smoke from the burning cocoa-nut shell, which will not rub off.

The inhabitants of Teste Island are an intelligent-looking people, and very friendly; they have large sailing canoes, with oval-shaped sails of various sizes, which they change according to the strength of the wind: the mast is formed with a tripod, two legs resting on the outrigger, and one on the bottom of the canoe; the ropes are made out of the bark of a tree twisted tightly together. The length of the largest canoe I saw was about thirty feet; they are decorated with a rough carving and the white cowrie shell, also with pieces of grass, flowers, &c. These islanders have, besides, smaller canoes, cut from the trunk of a single tree, with outriggers on one side only. These are whitewashed and ornamented with forms something like eyes in shape. On nearly every house we observed skulls hanging; I offered to buy one, but was refused in a very decided manner; they were probably not skulls of enemies, but rather those of relations.

On going to the top of the hill to look round, I found that the reef marked in the Admiralty chart was in reality a fine lagoon with apparently an excellent entrance at the south-east corner, and on the western side of East Island; I took a canoe and went out to see if the entrance was as good as it looked from the hill-top. On arriving I found there was a good-sized rock in the centre of the channel, on which the swell occasionally broke. It would, I think, however, make a good harbour for small vessels, but it requires entering by daytime until known, as there are several coral patches about it, besides the rock in the entrance.

We found the natives exceedingly pleasant and obliging; they are intelligent looking, and have that peculiar Jewish cast of features that one finds all along the north-east coast of New Guinea, and is without question of a higher type than that of the tribes on the south coast (Gulf of Papua), or those of the Calvados Chain, who are cannibals. It was at the last-named place that five hundred Chinamen (who were on their way to form a colony in New Guinea) were wrecked and eaten as required by the natives—at least all but three or four, who were bought back from the savages for looking-glasses, beads, &c.; but the circumstance is well remembered by many traders of the South Sea Islands.

We left Teste Island with regret, promising to return some day (which promise I fear will hardly be fulfilled now), and steered for Blanchard Island, where we came to anchor in the evening, off the northern point, very close to the shore. Next day we landed, when H—— succeeded in shooting the first duck I had seen in New Guinea; we took it on board thinking we had a great prize, and hung it up, telling the cook not to touch it, as I wanted to skin it. We then returned on shore to try and get its mate, but failed to do so, seeing the bird get up out of range.

On returning to the ship in the evening we found our beautiful duck plucked and cooked for our supper, and all the feathers carefully put in a bag; the cook triumphantly presented me with them saying, " Me no like you make work belong cook, massa; I take out all feathers belong bird, and put him in bag." The fellow had evidently thought that I wanted to pluck the duck myself and couldn't stand any interference in his department, and . thought he would take this opportunity of showing his disapproval; I felt very sad about it, and poor H—— was jumping mad. The duck was a white one, with grey head and dark grey bars on wings and tail, the beak yellow green; I have never seen another.   We left Blanchard Island next morning for China Straits, and had many canoes off to us from both sides of the straits—Hayter Island, as well as from Heath Island—bringing us many things for sale. Amongst them was a cuscus (a tree marsupial), a flying squirrel, and a small wallaby. The cuscus was a very handsome fellow, brown and white; they become quite tame, and we had several on board afterwards, where they lived a long time.   The flying squirrel is a pretty little creature, and will also become very tame if caught young.   The wallaby was of the same description as those found in New Britain and on the mainland of New Guinea. Full grown it stands about two feet six inches high; it is a dark brown colour, turning to white on the stomach and breast; it is very delicate, and will not live long in confinement—at least I have not been successful with them. We found that though there are plenty of pigs on this island they will not sell them, as they are the property of the women, who regard them much in the same light as their own children. I have seen one of these women hugging and caressing a pig more than ever she would have done one of her own babies.

The same evening we anchored off Heath Island (named after the President of the Marine Board and Harbour Master of Brisbane, Queensland, the same courteous gentleman to whom when in Brisbane we were indebted for so much kindness; he was, I believe, in these parts some years ago). Here we found that the natives brought off a description of sponge, which, though covered with a black film, speedily yields to a weak solution of muriatic acid, and turns out a really very presentable washing sponge.

We went on shore and tried to find the village marked on the Admiralty chart, but were not successful; I think it does not exist now, as we passed over the spot marked, and saw no trace of any house; we followed a small freshwater stream, hoping to find another duck, but were disappointed. We saw, however, several tracks of crocodiles, which seem to be pretty numerous here, though we did not actually come across one.

Many canoes came alongside our vessel with tortoiseshell and small black edge-pearl shell; we also bought a good many implements of war, tomahawks, spears, clubs, and shields.

The tomahawks are made of a stone very nicely

ground into somewhat the shape of a flat wedge, and beautifully smooth; some of them are from three to four inches across the widest part, which is ground to a sharp edge for cutting; the other end is jammed into a wooden handle, the part that holds the stone being formed of two pieces of wood lashed firmly round with split cane; the remainder of the handle is in the form of two sides of a right-angled triangle, the part for holding being the longest leg. These tomahawks are so formed that the harder the blow the more the stone is wedged into the handle. The largest size, I believe, being so unwieldy, is used merely for ornament. Some of them have the wooden holder movable, in order that the stone head may be turned to make an adze. The spears are varied in shape, those for fish having five or six hard betel-nut wood points, so lashed together into a handle that they spread out into a circle, distant about one and a half inches from each other, having one in the centre. Another fishing spear had two prongs barbed at the ends, carved out of the same piece of wood as the handle.

Of the fighting spears some are smooth-pointed but roughly made, others have many barbs, and are very neatly carved; they are made from various kinds of wood; the rougher ones appear to be of cocoa-nut wood—the others of a black wood like ebony, or a red wood that is much like the Fijian "greenheart." The clubs resemble swords in shape, some notched along the blade, others smooth, mostly made of betel-nut wood.

The paddles of the canoes are made of a light-coloured wood, with heart-shaped blades, the handle being about four feet long with a crutch-headed top, often very nicely carved into the shape of a bird. The shields are black, with white markings on them; they are about three feet long, and two broad, slightly curved at the sides; these are hung on the outrigger of the canoe, to form a bulwark, when fighting.

Some of the native ornaments are armlets, made of plaited cane dyed red; pieces of ground clam shell through the cartilage of the nose, which is pointed at the ends. The men often wear wigs, much in the same way that our young ladies wear fringes, only the native fringe can be pulled down over the chin to form whiskers. I noticed they did this several times when, having been paid for some article, they came back and asked to be paid a second time; however, this innocent ruse did not succeed more than once.

I noticed also necklets made of cassowaries' feathers, worked on to a cord, some also being made of bird of paradise plumes; these last they also wind round the uprights on the outriggers of their canoes for ornament. The waist-cloth is made of a bark of a tree, and is unornamented; whilst above the waist they wrap their bodies round and round with a description of black plaited cord, with bright yellow strands worked into it, which has something the appearance of a small snake. What the cord can be for I do not know; it cannot be only for ornament; it may be for catching turtle, but I hardly think it

is strong enough for one of any size. We also
bought a curious mask made of tortoiseshell which
is worn in dancing; it is ornamented with cassowaries' feathers, whitened round the eye-holes with

TORTOISESHELL MASK.
(*From Mt. Thompson, New Guinea.*)

lime, and coloured round the lips with red earth;
the nose-piece is fastened on, and the nostril holes
have pieces of pearl shell inserted. This mask, I was
informed by a native, comes from the mainland
(Mount Thompson).

All this time we had seen no women; I suppose it was too far for them to come in canoes.

Leaving Heath Island, we passed "Dinner" Island, and stood in for "Possession Bay" (Hayter Island), anchoring in seven fathoms water pretty close to shore.

Here an immense number of canoes came off to us; I do not think I exaggerate when I say that there were three hundred; two large fighting

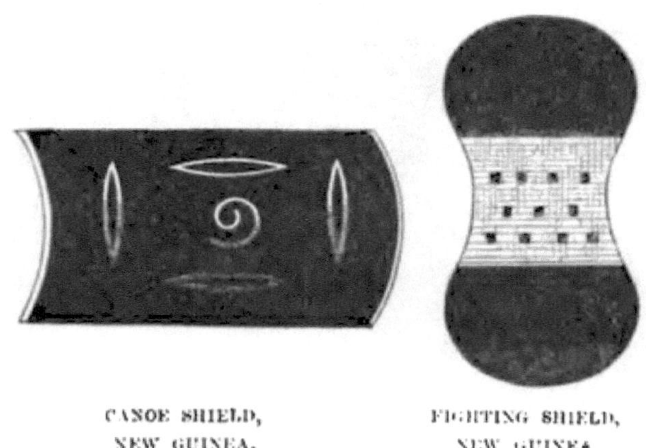

<table>
<tr><td>CANOE SHIELD,
NEW GUINEA.</td><td>FIGHTING SHIELD,
NEW GUINEA.</td></tr>
</table>

canoes cruised round outside the others, doubtless to keep the peace, as well as to intimidate us should we show any hostile intentions; the latter were very long, holding about thirty men each, the outriggers hung with shields, and bundles of spears. Here several women came out, paddled by their respective lords and masters (?). However, the grey mare appeared the better horse, as they abused and scolded the men if they did not keep close enough to the vessel's side to trade. When they did get alongside of

it, it was amusing to see how they settled down into
company manners, not giving way to eager excitement like the men, but sitting calmly in the canoes,
giving orders to the sterner sex what to sell and
what to take in exchange.

All barter goods that the men exchanged were
handed to the women, who examined them very
carefully, and then placed them under where they
were sitting. The women are evidently very clever
in the art of forcing trade. One lady had on a very
brightly-coloured grass petticoat, which we had some
delicacy in asking for. However, H—— mustered
up courage to point to it, upon which she shook
her head and pretended she could not sell it,
being ashamed to take it off; she, however, went so
far as to stand up and unfasten the string, then,
apparently being overcome by her modesty, sat
down again. This made H—— more urgent to get
it, so he showed her a tomahawk, upon which she got
up and took it off, and to our surprise had another
one underneath; thus by a piece of clever acting
getting double the price she would otherwise have
received, the other natives seeming to think it a good
joke. I must add that before this lady left she was
very anxious to part with her second petticoat, but as
we would not give the same price for it she had not
to sacrifice her modesty.

Possession Bay was taken " possession " of in the
Queen's name by Captain Moresby of the *Basilisk*
in 1873, at the time he discovered China Strait. On
a fine day this strait is a most beautiful passage, the

cleared green patches on the land, and the beautiful foliage coming down to the water's edge, with here and there a village surrounded with its groves of cocoa-nut palms, canoes hauled up on the beach or darting out from under the shadow of the trees, the natives that manned them wishing to intercept the vessel so as to have a look at the strangers, or else with something to sell.

There are the mountains rising at the back, with the signs of cultivation on their ample breasts; and as you pass close to the shore, the innumerable sounds of the woods become audible, the songs of the birds and the shouts of the natives, softened and harmonised by distance; above all there comes the indescribable perfume that seems to find its way into your very soul, the sweet odour of all the flowers and herbs, intermingled with the rich scent of the earth; it is in these unknown spots alone that nature is natural. Here you see no broken bottles or pieces of newspaper lying about —nothing in fact to mar the perfect beauty of the scene.

It surprises me much that some of those who own yachts do not visit these lovely haunts. One reads of cruises by these pleasure vessels to all parts of the civilised world in search of the beautiful, yet here, and indeed in all the Pacific Islands, is marvellous beauty unmarred since its creation. There, too, is the excitement of feeling that you may be (perhaps) the first white man that has set foot on this shore; and for those that like a little spice of danger thrown in (and where is the sailor, I may say the Englishman that does not ?), I would remind them that the natives are not all friendly, and although they may become so by fair dealing, treachery must be looked for at all times. Here is enterprise on which our yachtsmen may expend their energies; let them come here and discover new islands and new people. We Englishmen are far too apt to think that all parts of the world are discovered—we are much mistaken in this idea. There are hundreds, nay thousands of islands in the Pacific *never seen* by white men, save in the distance, and many, I have little doubt, never seen at *all*.

Only seven years ago I saw a small rock marked on the chart, and the sailing directions said it was reported to be a rock, but its existence was very doubtful. This *rock* was sixty miles out in the given longitude, it is true, but instead of *one rock* I found twenty-one islands and the finest race of inhabitants I have seen in these seas. What was most curious was that they had *no* weapons of war at all amongst them, only fishing spears, and such instruments as were necessary to maintain existence. They were most friendly, and gave us of the best they had; we in exchange leaving them two pigs, and probably now they have plenty of pork to eat, where before they had only fish, cocoa-nut, taro, yams, and land crabs.

Perhaps this is something that can hardly be credited by people in England, who see thousands of ships in their docks, and imagine they have sailed over every sea, and visited all the places of the earth; yet I have little doubt that there are many such islands still to be discovered in the Pacific Ocean.

New Guinea in itself, too, is an enormous field for discovery; the north-east coast is still comparatively unknown, and whereas it is delineated in the map as a straight, bold coast-line, it has in reality many beautiful harbours, and the scenery is truly grand.

I must apologise to the reader for thus leaving him alone in Possession Bay, whilst I have been wandering all over the Pacific; so now to return.

On leaving the Bay we ran past Mckinley Island, and thus leaving China Straits behind us, steered for Challis Head, and clear of China Rock, which has grown considerably larger since I saw it in 1875. The sand and broken coral have silted up all round what was once a small reef, and formed a sandbank. Moreover, we found what I feel sure was not in existence when I was here before, that is, two coral patches, with about two fathoms of water on them; this seems to show that the reefs are growing in this direction. A little further on, though, I found a shoal patch marked four fathoms, and on sounding found it still the same, so that seemingly some reefs grow much faster than others.

There is a very swift current at times through China Strait either way, ebb and flow, which may be favourable to the growth of reefs, and it seems to me certain that a strong current plays an important

part in their growth, from observations made elsewhere.

To the west of Mekinley Island lie Paples and
"Didymus" Islands, both good fields for the
entomologist and the bird collector, for there are
no natives living on them, yet he can always get
some to go with him from the other islands, to help
collect, if not afraid to trust himself in a canoe.

After Challis Head comes Negro Head, so called,
I imagine, from a round hillock on the coast, much
the shape of a negro's head, and the foliage on it,
which is short and thick, tending to increase the
resemblance. Negro Head is the northernmost
point of "Basilisk" Island, and after leaving it you
cross the mouth of Fortesque Strait; it was to the
north and east of this Strait that we sounded on the
coral patch marked four fathoms and obtained a
similar sounding.

From this we made for Mudge Bay, and anchored
just inside the western head, as the bay appeared
full of shoals, though ten fathoms of water was
marked in the chart.

We found the natives not nearly so quiet as those
of Hayter Island; they wanted to get on board, and
were inclined to be impertinent over their trading.
One man, more determined than the rest, got up out
of his canoe, reached over to the skylight, and stole
a knife that was lying on it; we did not see him, as
we were all busily engaged with the other natives,
but Master Pincher did, and caught hold of the
thief's hand, at the same time Rover had him by the

part of his body that was on the rail. The first we heard of it was a fearful howl from the man, who jumped about ten yards clear off the rail into the water. This made all the other natives laugh, and we got on better with them afterwards. The bitten native took the knife away with him, but did *not* come again to trade with us.

Natives in all parts of the South Seas do not consider thieving a fault; it is the being found out

NEW GUINEA CANOE, CHINA STRAITS.

that is the crime in their eyes, therefore when I occasionally made signs as of being bitten, and pointed to the land, the others would shake their heads, laugh, and wave their hands, expressing that the other would not come off again.

These natives use the same sort of weapons as those before described; they do a great deal of trading from island to island in their large canoes, the sails of which are oval in shape, something like a tea-tray, and are made of mats of cocoa-nut leaves. Of these they have three different sizes, a large one for fine weather, a small one for strong wind, and very small for a gale. In going about they have only to haul down the other end of the sail, and shift the steering paddle; they lie close to the wind and sail very fast.

Taking them on the whole the natives of these islands are a very friendly set, especially those on Teste, Basilisk, and Hayter Islands. I trust they may never become otherwise, but fear they will some day have to pass through the ordeal which all natives that have become intimate with whites have suffered—rebellion at first, then subjection, and at last entire extinction. White men will never become natives, natives cannot become white men, and of the two the weaker fails. This appears to be a most strongly illustrated law of nature throughout the vast regions of the South Seas.

CHAPTER II.

It was about six o'clock in the afternoon that we passed between Blakeny and Hull Islands and out into deep water beyond. Keeping on our course we steered to the eastward of Cape Ventenat to clear its dangerous reefs, and along the east coast of Normanby Island, with its rugged mountain peaks, crags, and chasms, a grand and broken outline. There must indeed have been a terrible convulsion of nature to have caused such an upheaval; it is a beautiful scene.

Leaving Cape Pierson we steered to pass between Jouveney and Jurien Islands, and suspecting a strong set from the eastward, I kept as far over in that direction as practicable to keep off the Luscanay Reefs, which extend from Welle Island north to Lagrandiere Island, with only a few passages through. I found that my suspicions were correct, as we were set to the westward of Jurien Island, passing between it and Trobriand Island.

The former presents a strange appearance, rising as it does to a considerable height in terraces one above the other, and looking as though it had been raised out of the sea in jerks, each terrace having at one time formed the sea beach. Jouveney Island, seen in the distance, appeared to be of the same formation, though it was too far off to see whether it was so.

Trobriand Island is low, and covered on the eastern side with what appeared to be iron bark trees, they having that peculiar spiked appearance that the foliage of this class of tree always has. The northernmost point of this island is Cape Denis, one hundred and eighty-two miles from Cape Orford in New Britain, about two days' sail, the Duke of York Islands being sixty-two miles from Cape Orford. We intended to make these islands our first stopping-place.

We actually passed Cape Orford in one day from Cape Denis, being carried along by the south-east monsoon, but as we passed Spacious Bay the breeze grew lighter, and at last fell altogether when we were about thirty miles south of the Duke of York Islands. That night it came on a fog with thick drizzling rain, such a thing I never saw again the whole time I was in these waters; but a fog we had, and a very thick one. About midnight we heard as we thought the sound of breakers, and there being no wind I was afraid the current must have set us on to the coast of Duke of York Island. The only chance to keep clear was to take to the sweeps, which we did, but too late, as we found ourselves in the middle of the break, which was rushing round with the most tremendous roar.

I shouted to Aleck to get the lead over the side

and see what water we had under us, and to the others to pull for their lives to get us clear. Forty fathoms and no bottom was the sounding given. This seemed so strange that I took the lead myself, and let out fifty fathoms and still no bottom, yet we heard breakers all round us, and just as if they broke in shallow water. This must be a tide rip I thought, and of no ordinary sort. I looked at the compass and found that the ship's head was going round and round; then I thought of whirlpools, &c., when suddenly the breakers ceased as suddenly as they had begun.

We were afterwards in several of these miniature whirlpools in this St. George's Channel, and from observation I have come to the conclusion that they are caused by the uneven formation of the bottom and the swiftness of the current over it, sometimes running at the rate of five or six knots in the direction of each monsoon.

The next morning we found ourselves to the north of Duke of York Islands, the current having drifted us thirty miles in the night. This will give some idea of the strength of these currents, which appear to be produced by the wind alone.

A German barque, the *Etienne*, was the best part of three months trying to beat a distance of twenty miles against the current. She would make a good start in the morning, when the monsoon began at about nine A.M., and would sometimes nearly reach her destination, but at sundown the wind always fell light, and back she would drift, further perhaps than she had come in the day. Therefore I would strongly advise any master coming *from* China this way during the south-east monsoon to go round the north of New Hanover, but through St. George's Channel if *going* there.

I can quote an instance of a large iron barque that we spoke in the St. George's Channel that took only thirteen days out from Newcastle, N.S.W., which was pretty good work, and this track I should certainly advise masters to take outwards in the S.E. and homewards in the N.W. monsoons, with clear water through St. George's Channel and to the north of New Britain.

By the way, I think this barque took us for a pirate, though we flew the British ensign, for she made sail as soon as she saw us, but as we were in the channel between Duke of York Island and New Ireland, and she was coming up it, I could have cut her off, whichever way she had headed ; when at last I hailed her they told me she was 13 days out from Newcastle, bound for China, and was going right on, not stopping. They might well be pardoned for taking us for pirates, for our deck was full of natives, quite naked or with only a piece of cloth tied round their waists or heads, and we white men did not present a very respectable appearance about that time. Besides this we had two little guns peeping over the sides, and being in such an out-of-the-way place we must have had altogether a rather sus-picious appearance. But I am running on talking about things that occurred after we had been in these waters some time, and we have not even arrived at New Britain yet.

Dampier, in 1699, was the first to decide that New Britain was a separate island from New Guinea, he having passed through those straits which are now called by his name, and which lie to the westward of New Britain and the eastward of Rooke Island. Some portions of the island were afterwards more exactly described by D'Urville, although this navigator visited it under very adverse weather. He gives it the native name of Birara, which I found to be the name also given to a part of the island some two hundred miles to the north-eastward of that portion which he describes—a circumstance which, I think, tends to prove that at some previous date the natives of the eastern and western ends of the island were connected, though at the present time their language, appearance, and customs are very different.

I was anxious to get to Nodup, a village just beneath the Mother Mountains in New Britian, that being my boy Aleck's home. I felt sure of finding friendly natives there, he having been kidnapped from this locality some years before.

However, we could only get near enough for a canoe to come off, and when they got alongside the natives were very surprised to see Aleck, as they had long since given him up, believing him to be dead. They asked him many questions about the others that had been taken with him, and he had to repeat that shameful story so often told, of how these poor natives, after being kidnapped by white men, were allowed to die like sheep on the wharf of a wealthy firm. They were housed in an old condemned deck-house on shore without windows and with a leaky roof, and this in the winter. There were eight at first, six of whom died on the wharf and one afterwards from the exposure. (The head of the firm on whose wharf the poor creatures perished passes for a very Christian man!) Aleck was the last of them, and he, I am glad to say, I was able to bring back to his own people. Poor fellow! when his countrymen began to talk to him he found that he had forgotten a great deal of the language, and could not answer them very well, having been away for five years. He found on asking for them that his father and mother were both alive, but living on an island called Matupi (in Blanche Bay) on the other side of the Mother Mountain.

As we could not get into Nodup, owing to the current setting north so strongly, I ran round Cape Stephens to anchor off the Goonan District, just the other side of the Cape, and out of the strong current. Here I found that I could get over the hills from Goonan to Blanche Bay, and thence to Matupi Island. So the next day Aleck, I, and some of the natives from the shore as guides, started off across the land, and found that it was only about twenty minutes' walk after all to get to the head of Blanche Bay, over one steep hill too, though the Admiralty charts make it at least four miles wide.

We found the land we passed through nearly all

cultivated, large crops of bananas, yams, and taro being all around us; the soil, too, seemed very rich, being formed of decomposed volcanic and vegetable matters.

Two villages that lay on our route struck me as being most remarkable for the neatness and taste with which the pieces of ground surrounding each house were laid out; the natives seemed to have collected from the bush a quantity of the brightest-looking variegated shrubs to plant round their dwellings, though this I found afterwards was done as much to save trouble as to look ornamental, as they use the bright leaves, &c., in their dances, and it is convenient to have them handy.

The houses are for the most part made of bamboo thatched with the pandannas leaves, and are not very high, with the exception of that belonging to the chief, which is generally a considerably larger build-ing. The natives have a bad habit of making fires inside their huts, which is a pity, as if it were not for the dirt from the smoke they would not be bad at all; the strong smell, too, of the burnt wood is objectionable; but taken as a whole, the appearance of a Goonan village is very pretty.

The sleeping bunks, as I will call their beds, are generally made of the sides of a canoe split off and laid on posts driven into the ground; on them are laid mats, made of green cocoa-nut leaves, which, although very cool, are rather rough, as they leave part of the thick stem on them. One of these mats is always brought out for a visitor, followed by a native with the inevitable betel-nut, which you must chew or give offence.

As we passed over the top of the hill we had a grand view of the Mother Mountain and South Daughter, with Blanche Bay and the shore on the far side of it; under the Mother we could see the volcano with its dense volumes of smoke and steam.

After crossing the hill the road descended all the way to the beach, along which we had to walk about a mile and a half to get a canoe, which, after a lot of haggling, Aleck made arrangements for hiring, to take us over to Matupi Island.

Going along the shore we passed one freshwater creek, and another of hot water, which, being at a temperature of about 120 Fahrenheit, was unpleasantly hot to the bare feet. This creek appeared to have no particular source inland, but was rather a shallow crater with one side open to the bay. The whole shore is covered with pumice-stone, and the natives told me they had a terrible eruption about twelve years ago, in which many men were killed by the falling of huge blocks of pumice-stone, and that there had been several smaller outbursts since.

The canoe we had secured was a good-sized one, paddled by two women and a man; these, with Aleck and myself as passengers, made up all hands.

About this time I began to feel that terrible languor which is a precursor of fever and ague, and had to lie down in the canoe on some cocoa-nut mat baskets they had with them; so, unfortunately, could not take as much notice of our surroundings as I wished to do. We passed about a quarter of a mile from the two remarkable rocks known as the Beehives, the largest of which, though rising perpendicularly out of the sea for about two hundred feet, has on it quite a thriving village of fishermen. I also noticed several cocoa-nut trees growing apparently on the bare face of the rock, clinging to it with their roots as a parasite plant does to the trunk of a tree. These rocks lie east by north of Matupi about a mile and a quarter.

Matupi Island is evidently formed by volcanic agency, as there is an extinct crater in the centre, now partly filled up, and most of the island is sand and pumice-stone.

It is covered with cocoa-nut trees and thickly populated. On landing I was too much exhausted with fever to go even as far as the house of a half-caste trader who was living on the island, so lay down in one of the open canoe sheds on the beach. Here I had quite a large audience to see the " white man " who had brought back " Etugerier " (Aleck's native name). They brought me some green cocoa-nuts, which were very refreshing; and in about an hour's time, the shaking fit having passed off, I started across the island to the trader's house.

Let me now describe this fever for the information of those who do not know its nature or do not appreciate its virulence. No man escapes it that travels much on shore in these islands; I first got it long ago in New Guinea, so that it was not new to me. The first symptoms generally are these: an aching in the legs, and a tired feeling generally, then the eyes begin to hurt, and lastly your back feels cold, and shivers go through and through the body, although your skin feels burning hot. You then pile on blankets, but cannot get warm for some time; when you do you feel hotter and hotter, and perspiration pours off the body till everything is wet. Off go the blankets then, which is a bad thing, as doing so drives the fever in again; great thirst is then usually felt, and when the heat is passed you fall asleep as a rule, thoroughly worn out, and on waking feel weak and shaky.

The fever begins generally as an intermittent, and as it becomes more settled in the body, a *remittent*, perhaps every other day; at last the shivers do not come at all, but instead, heavy vomiting and cough. This is the last stage, and if you do not then get away from the climate it will prove fatal.

Many white men I have seen with it have taken so much quinine that the remedy has been almost worse than the disease, for in one case that I had special knowledge of, the poor fellow took so much that he lost the use of his left eye altogether. I myself have frequently lost my hearing for some days, and found my memory confused through the same cause, too much quinine; for in order to kill this fever, such large doses are needed that they injure the system almost as much as the fever itself.

By far the most useful medicine for it is citrate of iron and strychnine; one of strychnine to one hundred of iron, taken in doses five grains to an ounce of water. This has never failed where the case was not too far advanced, and in some cases made a cure when continued with ; and it would, I feel sure, keep fever *away* almost entirely if taken twice a day before any symptoms are felt.

You will never catch this fever if you are as much as a quarter of a mile even from the shore, nor *on* the shore even if you keep clear of mangrove swamps and thick forests. Only stick to the iron, and avoid all spirits ; their use is certain death in such a climate as most of these islands possess ; a little wine now and then is a good thing with your meals, or light beer. Any one feeding well, and keeping up strength in this way, is less likely to catch the fever than one who lives poorly and overtaxes his strength.

One thing I omitted to say, viz., that white women seem to stand this climate better than white men, as an instance : a missionary's wife I have the pleasure of knowing has never had fever, though she has been many years in the South Seas, while her husband has had it many times. I must also mention that thin people seem less liable to it than stout ones. My advice is, do nothing that can possibly weaken the body, and don't take quinine.

Now back again to Matupi. I stayed with the trader that night, and next morning he was kind enough to assist me in purchasing some pigs from the natives. I got three very fine ones for a tomahawk a piece, the tomahawks cost tenpence (retail)—a very cheap pig ! They are all fed on cocoa-nuts, and the flesh has something of the flavour of the nut to the taste, which is to my mind very pleasant.

The trader's house is a weather-boarded, framed one, roofed with corrugated iron, and divided into three compartments; the front door opens into the general room, where we took our meals, &c. On one side was a door opening into the bedroom, and on the other a door into the trade-room, where all the stock-in-trade is kept.

Each room was furnished, though roughly; the sitting-room having a deal table, two chairs, and a roughly-made couch; the bedroom a trestle-bed and a chest of drawers; whilst the trade-room possesses merely shelves all round for the various goods, &c.

Each room has one window, furnished with wooden shutters in case of an attack from the natives; the first room has also a door at the back, for communication with the kitchen, a native built house some yards away from the main building; the cooking arrangements being of the most simple order. Near by is the copra-house, a large building of native construction (bamboo and thatched), to which is fixed a strong door, kept padlocked. Here is kept the copra bought from the natives, ready cut and dried, and placed there till a ship comes to take it; the houses being obliged to be strongly built and kept locked, or the natives would steal the copra and sell it to the trader over again.

I suppose there are but few English people outside the trade who know what copra is; I will therefore explain:—it is the white pith of the ripe cocoa-nut

cut into strips and dried in the sun. This is brought to
the trader in baskets, varying from three to twenty
pounds in weight; the payment at the time of which
I am speaking was a thimbleful of beads for each
pound of copra, though this alters as time goes on
and more traders come to make opposition. The nut
is full of oil, and on reaching Europe the copra is
crushed in mills, and the oil pressed from it. This is
cocoa-nut oil, and it can be now so well manipulated
that half the oil sold as "olive oil" is really from
the cocoa-nut. The refuse is made into oil-cake, for
feeding and fattening cattle. The value of copra
in the English market varies from about £10 to £16
per ton. The traders are very rarely trading for
themselves, but for a firm who send ships now and
then to fetch the copra, and supply the traders with
provisions; and for the work the traders sometimes
receive a salary and sometimes are paid about £2 per
ton. Others, again, receive their money in both
ways, that is, a small salary, and receive also a rate
of perhaps three dollars per ton of their copra.

Trade is not limited to their copra; traders also
get tortoise-shell, pearl-shell, candle-nuts, and the
bark of a tree called "fowbash," which is to send to
Europe to be manufactured into paper. For all these
things they get small sums allowed them; but then
they have to buy all their provisions from the ships
at very dear rates; and though their trade is supplied
to them, they have to give an account of the way in
which it is expended.

It is not an easy matter to be a good trader, and

some who go to the South Sea Islands are not at all fitted for the post. It requires a man to have a cool judgment and great tact in dealing with the natives; he also ought to know what to do, and at the right moment, in the event of a dispute arising whilst trading. The trader I visited at Matupi was the first that had been able to stay on the island, two others having been driven off, in fear for their lives: but the one now there appears to have great influence with the people, and to be liked as well as feared.

That is the great secret in getting on well with the natives, you *must* be feared as well as liked. If you are *liked* only (as missionaries try to be), their avarice gets the better of their liking, and they will murder you on the very first opportunity, for the sake of some small possession they covet. But if they *fear* you as well, then they will not be very likely to attack you, lest they should come to harm themselves; and, liking you, will bring you anything they have to sell.

Each trader as a rule has a boat, in which he goes round to the villages to collect and buy copra, tortoise-shell, &c., manned by a native crew, to each of whom they pay a stick of tobacco a day, or a clay pipe. The trader very often depends upon the chief to provide him with men, to whom he also pays something. The boat is generally kept in a boathouse on the beach, of native construction, to prevent the sun from warping and cracking it.

The whole of the trader's house and outbuildings

are surrounded by a palisade, made of strong bamboo lashed together, and this is a " trading establishment " as it exists in New Britain. Should I have to refer to traders again, the reader will now understand all about them.

From this house I could observe the volcano more closely than before, as it seems to tower up just above the island, though in reality it is quite a mile distant from the base. The crater is not very large, and has several cavernous outlets, through which the steam and smoke escape; not to any very large extent in dry weather, but the volume is much increased in the rainy season.

There appears to be a good deal of sulphur in the crater, the nearest wall of which is broken away, so that from Matupi one can see well into it. The mountain itself appears to be formed of decayed pumice-stone, partly overgrown with small bushes and grass, and is, I should say, about one thousand feet high.

There is good anchorage between the mainland and Matupi on this side, having the Mother Mountain on a line with the centre of Matupi, and about two and a half cables length from the island.

On leaving Matupi I determined to return to Goonan by another route, longer, but very interesting. I landed in the northernmost bight of Great Harbour, on low, flat, marshy land, sparsely covered with stunted trees ; the ground is thick with rotten pumice, overgrown with grass.

Here I saw the New Britain quail, a small bird

about the size of a three weeks' old chicken. It lies very close in the grass, and when disturbed springs up with a whirring noise not unlike a miniature pheasant. The flight is short and quick, and the bird affords good sport with the gun, and is very nice eating, though you have to get a good many to make a meal.

We (*i.e.*, my guides and I) passed over about a mile of this sort of country, and gradually ascended, the trees becoming thicker and more stately as we advanced, till at last we came to a steep ascent, beautifully covered with palms, other trees, bananas, and dracœnas, all growing in wild luxuriance.

We walked over the low range that extends from the noble Mother to her scarcely less stately North Daughter; then rapidly descending, passed through a smooth though sloping tract of land, which was so hollow that it sounded like walking on the roof of a house, and is quite hot from the subterraneous fires, though, strange to say, grass and other herbs grow here quite luxuriantly. I must say I should not care to live in this place, for even walking on it makes one feel nervous, lest it should give way and you should be precipitated into the abyss.

We came, after crossing this volcano trap, on to the beach, and on walking along it a short distance southward reached Nodup. This village is situated just under the Mother on the north side. The name of the chief of Nodup is Torrortooroo, and a very fine man he is. At one time he was a bitter enemy to the white men; but being gifted with common sense above that of his countrymen, he found it was the best policy to be friendly with them, and if possible to help the whites in any quarrel with the natives of his districts or with other tribes.

Thus he has become a very powerful chief, and is a firm supporter of the white men. In the course of conversation he said to me, "One time I did not know what the white man was. I thought he was the devil, and I did not want him in my country. But now I know if I kill one white man, ten more will jump up and kill me. The white man has plenty of guns, plenty of ball and powder. Why should I fight against him? He is my friend, and I am his; he has big ships, guns, powder, ball, and beads, and everything my countrymen want; why should I drive him away and hurt myself?" This is a literal translation of what he said. I told him in reply that I should tell my countrymen what he said, and that I felt sure that any of them that came in this direction would be glad to meet so good a friend. I then asked him about a house, and where he thought would be the best place for going inland, and he recommended Kininigunun as most suitable. He provided canoes for our return to Goonan, which we safely accomplished in the evening, taking the pigs with us; Aleck staying behind with his father and mother, relating, no doubt, wonderful stories of how the white men live, &c.

A few days after he came off with another lad who had hurt his arm. Aleck, it appears, had bought a gun in Sydney with some of the money I had given him; he loaded this gun to shoot at a pigeon, but did not, however, discharge it, lying down to sleep instead. His brother saw another bird, loaded the gun again, but did not fire, and left the double-loaded gun lying by Aleck; then this other man came up, and, loading the gun a third time, fired; the result can be imagined; the gun burst, and the man was badly wounded in the arm: he was lucky to escape with so light an injury.

I doctored up his arm for him, for which he wanted to pay me in native money. I did not of course wish to take it, but Aleck told me I had better do so, as there is an idea amongst these people that if they do not pay they do not get well. What a pity for our medical profession that the same superstition is not more prevalent amongst us!

CHAPTER III.

FROM Goonan we sailed to Duke of York Island, where I heard there was now a mission-station erected, with a missionary of the name of Brown at the head of it. We were carried a good deal N. by the current after leaving Cape Stephens, but getting under the lee of Duke of York Island, we found that by making short tacks we could work up very well indeed, and I am inclined to think there must be an eddy-current setting back towards Duke of York Island; we anchored in Makada Harbour, off Makada Island. Duke of York Island is about five miles in length E. and W., by three and a half miles N. and S., and Makada Island lies to the extreme north of Duke of York, with two more small islands, Myet Islands, again to the eastward. These three, with the northern coast of Duke of York, form Makada Harbour, better known to traders as Ferguson's Harbour.

This is a pretty fair harbour during the S.E. monsoon, but it cannot be considered first-rate, owing to the very strong currents that sweep through the narrow channels between the islands, and the inferior holding ground, which is mostly white, shifting sand, with a varying depth of water from three to ten fathoms.

We here had a visit from the trader in charge of Hernsheim and Co.'s station, Mr. Blohm, who thought that we were a schooner he expected. After we had returned his visit and seen his station, which is really a very fine collection of buildings (though in an unhealthy place), we landed on Duke of York Island, and crossed the very narrow spit of land (about two hundred yards) which divides Makada Harbour from Port Hunter.

This is a beautiful little bay, surrounded by white beach, with cocoa-nut trees thrusting their long stems over the still blue water, and there is a cluster of houses in the bight at Mowlott, with dense bush behind. The land rises on each side of the bay to the height of about one hundred feet, covered with many-hued plants and creepers, flitting over which are the brightly-coloured birds and butterflies. This, with the tropical blue sky above all, forms one of those lovely visions that are retained by the mind all one's life.

The ground rises all the way to Mr. Brown's house, which is situated at the summit of the hill, on the north side of the bay, overlooking that portion of St. George's Channel which lies between Duke of York and New Ireland, the side of the hill facing the channel dropping sheer down to the sea one hundred feet or more. We found Mr. Brown at home, who, with his good lady, made us welcome to a meal of somewhat native fare, though there was that which we had not tasted since leaving Australia, a good loaf of bread.

He asked us for all the news of the civilised world, which of course is like another world to him here, as he can only get news when some mission vessel arrives (the great event), once a year. Mr. Brown has employed his spare time in making a very fine collection of birds from Duke of York Island, New Britain, and New Ireland; he has also some few beetles and butterflies, but not many.

Port Hunter was first visited by Captain Hunter, a whaler; he was also, I believe, the first to find out that New Britain and New Ireland were separate islands, for it was before supposed that St. George's Channel was only a deep bay, and indeed it very much presents this appearance from the southward as you come up the channel.

There was a whaling station formed here for preparing the oil for shipment, and the look-out place was on nearly the same spot as that on which Mr. Brown's new house is to be built, a little higher up the hill than the site of his present residence. A trading station too was started afterwards, but was burnt by the natives, who had quarrelled with the trader.

The mission had been there three years at the time of my visit, and I cannot speak very favourably of the progress it had made, though it was from no

want of zeal on the part of the missionaries themselves, but rather from lack of sympathy in the
natives, who do not appear to take much interest in
learning anything, except perhaps a new dance.
The first two or three times " lotu" or religious service
is held at any fresh place, members come down to
see what it is like ; after that they seem to get tired
of it, and stay away. I asked an old chief one day
if he had been to lotu, and how he liked it. " Well,"
said he very seriously, " I went to sleep, but it was not
at all comfortable. I don't think I shall go again."
Going to sleep in church, however, is *not* peculiar to
savages ! I do not think there are ten *real* converts
amongst the Duke of York natives.

From Makada Harbour we sailed S.W. for the
northern entrance of Mioko Harbour, which is said
to be a very fine one; it is really very convenient,
having one entrance bearing N.W. and another S.E.,
which enables a vessel to make use of it in either
monsoon to come in and go out with a fair wind.
On leaving Makada Harbour the first headland you
pass is Peninsular Point, a curious little hillock
jutting out into the water by itself, with only a low
neck of sand joining it to the mainland ; the next
being Rukukuroo Point, then a straight piece of coast,
with shallow water extending some distance from it,
belted with cocoa-nut trees, and every here and there
a native house. Rukukuroo Point is the next,
rising suddenly from the sea with a nasty reef lying
off it, about E. three-quarters, S. one mile, with also
another reef, to the northward of it again, about

half a mile, bearing from Kukukuroo Point E. by N.

Foul Bay is a wide one full of patches and rocks; and then you get to the northern entrance to Mioko Harbour, which is between Ulu Island and a small but somewhat elevated island off the coast of Duke of York.

There are no inhabitants in Ulu Island, but there are a large quantity of wild pigs on it; the small island on the other side is also uninhabited, but is used as a sort of half-way house for canoes going to and from Makada, Port Hunter, &c.

Next to Ulu Island lies Utuan Island—this is spelt Outan on the Admiralty charts; why, I do not know, as Outan can never sound like U-t-u-a-n ; indeed, I am not at all sure it should not be spelt *Utuwan*, so very pronounced is the *an*. I think particular care should be taken to get the native names as nearly correct as possible, as it is of great assistance in communicating with the natives, and saves much trouble in other ways; no native, I feel sure, would understand the name of Outan, as they are not quick at understanding roughly pronounced words.

The natives of this island are troublesome and dangerous. On one occasion, having to do some repairs to my vessel, I grounded her on the sand-spit lying to the eastern extremity of Utuan, and wanting a piece of land for my work on shore, I sent for the chief and bought about an acre with a house on it just opposite where the vessel lay.

I then told him that if the things I brought on

shore were left alone, and not tampered with by the natives, that I would return him the land, and give him a present. This seemed to satisfy him thoroughly, and he promised that it should be all right, and that he would taboo the ground, that is, he would not allow any one to come on except those I required to help me. This went on very well for a short time, but at last I began to miss small things, and one morning H—— came to me and told me that during the night some of the natives had cut the bellows of the forge through at the nozzle. This of course was irreparable, and foolishly I went on shore by myself to see about it.

I found the chief not far off, and I said to him, "One of your people has broken my bellows, you must make him pay for it" (this is the native custom to pay in shell money (dewarra) for any mischief they may do, even to killing a man). He answered me in that impudent manner the natives know so well how to assume : "I do not know anything about it, and I do not mean that any one shall pay for it." I answered, "You *will* find out who did it, and they *shall* pay for it. I came on your land by your own consent; I have given you presents, and your men have stolen from me and I have not spoken; now I mean to have payment for this."

As I spoke I looked round, and found about fifty armed men coming out of the bush behind me. Hallo! thought I, this looks like fighting ; so I began to back down to the beach, at the same time preparing a small revolver I had in my pocket. The old chief meanwhile had taken a tomahawk and spear from behind a tree, and made a rush for me, and as he lifted his tomahawk to strike I fired full at his breast, but the revolver missed fire, and I only saved my skull by catching his arm as it fell, and giving him a trip at the same time, which enabled me to back away faster than he could follow me.

It was not safe to turn and run, as then I could not see to ward off any spears they might throw; but as the chief was making for me the second time, one of the others threw a spear, which I avoided by knocking it off with my hand; however, it pierced it below the first finger. Then the chief made another rush for me, and as he struck I fell backwards over the root of a tree. I tried then to fire the revolver, and it would not work, but at that moment I heard a rushing noise in the leaves and a howl from the chief. My old dog Rover had him by the leg, in which he made his teeth meet, but he did not stop long enough to let the man get a blow at him, and though the natives threw many spears, they could not hit him; he was too quick for them.

Rover's timely assistance enabled me to get down to the beach and call H——, who jumped ashore with the muskets. The natives, however, had cleared off into the bush, and I am glad to say we had no occasion to use them. I sent then for Torrortooroo, who came over with his canoes, and when they saw I meant business they came to terms, and paid the fine, one hundred fathoms of dewarra. Then I made the chief a present, he made me one, and we were good friends again. Since my return to England I hear they have killed Mr. Klienschmit and two Frenchmen on this same island. Mr. Klienschmit was a naturalist collecting for the museum of Messrs. Godefroy. However, I believe the natives received a severe lesson for his murder. It was a narrow escape for me, and taught me that it is unwise to go alone unarmed amongst the natives; they always carry arms themselves, so will despise and take advantage of any one without, especially in the case of a quarrel.

My hand gave me much trouble for some time afterwards, indeed I was almost afraid the spear had been poisoned, but fortunately it was not. They poison their spears by dipping them into a putrefied dead body; and though this does not last long on the spear it is very deadly while it does.

You have now some idea of what these natives are like; it would have been a very bad thing to have gone away and left the quarrel unsettled, as they would have attributed it to cowardice, and told other natives that they had driven me away. This would have led to others attempting the same thing elsewhere; and this is also why it is so difficult to wait for the coming of a man-of-war or other authority to arbitrate.

The next island to Utuan eastward is Mioko, after which the harbour is named; on it is the head station of Messrs. Godefroy and Sons for these islands. It is a curious-looking island, in shape something like the dried tongues one sees in grocers' shops; there is a little cove or creek running up into the bush with water deep enough for small vessels to anchor in if they wish to be sheltered from the wind. On this island Mr. Klienschmit and his wife had their house; the natives are friendly and thoroughly accustomed to white men.

Mioko Harbour is really a very good sheltered harbour, with fine anchorage and holding ground, the only disadvantage being a nasty piece of foul ground in the centre, with rocks showing at low springs; the rise and fall is about three feet, but it greatly depends on the strength of the wind.

On the coast of Duke of York, and immediately before coming to the eastern entrance of the harbour, is a creek running a considerable distance inland, on one side of which fresh water is obtainable. The eastern entrance to the harbour is between Mioko and a small rocky island that is nearly steep to, therefore on going out or coming in keep the small island well aboard, for there is shoal water on the Mioko side.

To the south of Mioko Harbour lies another small one enclosed by the islands Kerawara and Kubokonilik, and the reefs attached to them; it affords good shelter for small vessels. On leaving Mioko we coasted along Duke of York Island, and when off Weira Point a canoe came out with the chief of that place in it, Lip-lip by name, who wanted to sell some tortoise-shell.

He is a great rogue and an inveterate cannibal,

though he denies it most determinedly, as do all the natives of Duke of York who have had sufficient intercourse with white men to know that the latter do not approve of cannibalism.

The people of Weira are great travellers, going long distances in their canoes, which are different from the small coasting ones, having no outrigger and being built much in the shape of a whale-boat. sharp at both ends. The planks are all lashed together and on to the ribs, and the lower part is hewn out of a single piece of wood, into which the ribs are fixed and lashed to keep them in.

All the seams and crevices of any kind are filled with the kernel of a nut, grated very fine and pressed into the holes. This in time gets quite hard, indeed it is easier to break the wood than wrench a joint apart.

The canoes are very neatly made, and I think the natives must have learnt the art of building them from the Solomon islanders, for the canoes much resemble those made by the latter people. Some whites have told me that the idea was taken from the whalers' boats, but I feel sure this is not the case, as these natives are not at all inventive out of their own groove.

After leaving Weira Point we reached Port Hunter, where we anchored.

The natives of the Duke of York group appear to be a mixture of the inhabitants of New Britain and New Ireland. I fancy at some former date a tribe from New Britain must have been driven off

VILLAGE, DUKE OF YORK ISLAND.

To face page 51.

the mainland (probably from Birara) and colonised the Duke of York group, beginning at the southern-most end, where they appear to be the original inhabitants, and still hold intercourse with Birara. Then it is probable that they went over to New Ireland to trade for provisions, and eventually bought wives there; this I imagine to be the case, as the Duke of York language more closely resembles that of Birara than that of New Ireland, though the New Ireland natives seem to understand Duke of York dialect, unlike as it is to their own language. When speaking of New Ireland I of course refer to that part immediately opposite Duke of York group. In parts of this group, too, the women have a custom of covering the loins, which custom only belongs to New Ireland, seeming to point to the fact that the women must have come from thence and continue the same practice; the men go entirely naked.

I cannot say that I found much more intelligence amongst these natives than in either of the other islands, and though Mr. Brown has chosen it as his head mission-station, it was probably more for its central position than from any intellectual supe-riority in the natives. The men are very well-built, sturdy fellows, of medium height (about 5 ft. 8 in.) and dark skinned, though by no means black, the skin of a healthy native having a rich copper tinge. They do not allow their hair to grow to any great length (as in New Guinea); it is in-clined to be woolly, though not so much so as that of an African.

A practice prevails among them of covering the hair with lime, which turns it a light tawny red; I never remember having seen a bald man or woman unless they were shaved, which is sometimes the case when in mourning for a relative, and the head is then blackened with charcoal and oil, or sometimes for sanitary reasons.

The women when young are well-made and upright, but as they grow older get, from the immense burdens they carry, an unnatural stoop, which they afterwards retain, whether carrying or not; they also age very quickly, which may be partly the effect of the climate, but perhaps is more from the ill-treatment they receive at the hands of the men, who look upon them as quite inferior beings, only existing for their pleasure and profit. The women work in the yam patches to prepare them for planting, they turn up the ground with sharp sticks, and burn all the grass and weeds, they then plant in the tubers which, when grown, the men condescend to get up.

Women also do most of the marketing, the men as a rule only accepting the payment.

There is a very disagreeable skin disease amongst these natives, which indeed prevails all over the islands; it is called "Buckwar," and attacks a great number; it consists in a peeling off of the skin, sometimes all over the body, sometimes in one part only, and appears to be hereditary, though in the young children it does not show until they are about three or four years old; and those who have it do not seem to be inconvenienced in any way, except that they are continually scratching. The natives attribute it to inoculation from a poisonous plant that grows in the bush, but Mr. Brown told me that he had treated it with partial success by giving sulphur and rubbing flour of sulphur on to the parts affected. This would give one the idea that it was a kind of scabies, though in my own mind I connect it with the total absence of salt in their food. It does not appear to be catching to white men, and though whites have said to me that they have caught it, the sores on examination did not appear to be the same thing, but were brought on by eating too much pork and by the heat of the climate.

Moreover, these sores soon disappear from the white man's skin, whereas the natives never lose them, the only *partial* recovery even being that mentioned by Mr. Brown.

The native money in New Britain consists of small cowrie shells strung on strips of cane, which in Duke of York is called "dewarra." It is measured in lengths, the first length being from hand to hand across the chest with the arms extended; second length from the centre of the breast to the hand, one arm extended, and the third from the shoulder to the tip of the fingers along the arm; fourth, from the elbow to the tip of the fingers; fifth, from the wrist to the tip of the fingers; and the sixth, finger lengths. Fish are generally bought by their length in dewarra unless they are *too* small. A large pig will cost from thirty to forty lengths of the first measure, and a small one ten.

The dewarra is made up for convenience into coils of one hundred fathoms or first lengths; sometimes as many as six hundred fathoms are coiled together, but not often, as it would be too bulky to remove quickly in case of an invasion or war, when the women carry it away to hide; these coils are very neatly covered with wicker work, like the bottom of our cane chairs. If asked where the shells came from the natives will tell you that they do not know; but several of the chiefs do, and it is from a place called Nukani, a considerable distance down the north-west coast.

The shells are buried in the earth to bleach them, after which they are tapped with a stone on the top, which breaks a small hole; they are then strung on strips of cane; this last process is, I believe, done by the chiefs alone.

The measurement of the shell-money is the same in New Britain as here, though it is called by another name (taboo). At Mioko and Utuan they use another kind of money as well as this, the other being made of a little bivalve shell, through which they bore a hole and string it on pieces of native-made twine; it is also chipped all round till it is about a quarter of an inch in diameter, and then smoothed down into even discs with sand and pumice-stone. This is of no use in Duke of York Island, but is eagerly asked for in Birara (another connecting link between the south of Duke of York and that district of New Britain).

The arms the natives carry are nearly all imported from New Britain or New Ireland. They used to have the stone tomahawk before the white man's iron "trade" tomahawks became so plentiful; this they fix on to a long handle (about four feet long) with carved ornaments at the end, and below the blade on the handle they cut notches to signify the number of men they each have killed. Polygamy prevails here, and any man that has much dewarra can have as many wives as he feels inclined to purchase. The most I ever saw was eight, I think, and the man seemed to have a great difficulty in managing them. The only way he did so was by the aid of a big stick, which he used pretty freely, judging by the screams that were frequently heard when near enough to his enclosure.

There are several chiefs to Duke of York, the greatest, that is to say the most powerful, is Tor Poulo; he is king of the greater part of Duke of York, and he also has possessions in New Britain and New Ireland. This chief goes amongst the whites by the name of "King Dick."

I shall never forget his coming on board the first time; he came off in a small canoe paddled by two of his wives. H—— said to me, "Who in the world is this gentleman?" He had on a stove-pipe hat somewhat the worse for several crushings and a red flannel shirt.

He happened also to be in mourning for one of his

wives, and was therefore blackened with charcoal and oil all over his face and head.

When he came alongside, H—— asked him what he wanted. "I am King Dick," he said, coming on board. "Where is the captain of this vessel?" (he spoke really very good English). When I was pointed out to him as the captain, he came aft to me, and again introduced himself with so much real hauteur and grace that, in spite of his ridiculous appearance, I could not help admiring him.

But the spell was soon broken, when he began to beg for tobacco and pipes, in fact anything he saw that pleased him; we became very good friends, and I always had a friendly reception from him when I paid him a visit on shore.

But he was a very crafty, subtle, and in fact one of the best of native statesmen; indeed he would hardly have held his large possessions against his numerous enemies had he not been what he was.

Next in importance is Tora-good (I forget his native name), which is a corruption of thorough-good, the name given him by whites.

His country is Rukukuroo, and extends for a considerable distance inland; he is a terrible old cannibal. I have myself seen the disjointed limbs of a man hanging near his house on a tree that is tabooed for that purpose.

Mr. Brown went to him one day to expostulate with him on having a body hanging up near his house, to be sold in joints; and he answered by saying, "What can I do? that man helped to eat my mother!"

He knows that cannibalism is abhorrent to white men, so is ashamed to speak to one of them about it. The practice once having been started, I suppose it is almost impossible for these poor creatures to give it up, so great is their desire for human flesh, and cannibalism has existed in these islands no one knows how long.

They prefer taking their victims alive in order to torture them. One poor fellow was taken so from a small village situated inland (in Duke of York Island) that had been attacked; he managed to escape, but was unfortunately caught again; they then cut off his feet, burning the stumps of his legs to prevent his bleeding to death, and so took him to the place where they intended to eat him; happily the poor fellow died before they could torture him any further.

This was not done by Tora-good, though I cannot say he has not done something of the same sort; yet this man, when first I visited him, was fondling one of his children in his arms and two more were playing about his knees, a perfect picture of domestic happiness. He called to his wife to bring out mats for me to sit on, and then came the inevitable betel-nut; after which he talked to me in such a fond parental manner about his children that I found it hard to believe that such a man could be guilty of the awful crime of cannibalism.

He made me a present of a fine pig, and I gave

him some red cloth and beads for his wives and children, and a knife, a tomahawk, and tobacco and pipes for himself; he took me to see some dewarra he had just been paid by another district, to prevent his going to war with them, about four hundred fathoms. When he began to talk about fighting his whole manner changed so completely that he no longer seemed to be the same man; the wild beast look came into his eyes, which I have always noticed when the natives only *speak* of such things; but alas! what can one expect of men who devour each other like wild animals?

The next chief in importance is Lip-lip, chief of Weira; he is an old man and a big villain, not to be trusted, though he pretends to be a great friend of the white man; and after him Warroowarrum, who is King Dick's brother, and chief of Port Hunter and the Tobaran canoe.

King Dick is chief of the Duk-duk, from which he gains much of his power, both of which things, the Tobaran canoe and the Duk-duk, I will describe later on. There are many other minor chiefs in Duke of York, but they are in reality subject to the greater ones.

On the death of one of the chiefs the eldest nephew on the sister's side always succeeds his uncle, as they remark with some sense, " that a man may always know who his mother is, but not always his father." So should the eldest sister not have any children, the eldest son of the second sister succeeds, and so on.

Should there be no descendant at all, the people of that district elect a new chief, generally choosing an individual for his wealth, as that constitutes the sinews of war, and they choose the one who can pay them best for fighting.

The Duk-duk, of which Tor Poulo is chief, may be spoken of as the administration of law, being

THE DUK-DUK.

judge, policeman, and hangman all in one, as he settles all disputes and punishes all offenders.

This mysterious power is in reality *one* man, appointed by the chief, and who is dressed in leaves, which cover his body to below the waist ; he wears a large helmet, coming completely over the face and resting on the shoulders, in shape like an extinguisher.

This is made of net-work, so that he can both breathe and see without being seen ; it is painted to represent a hideous face. This strange figure travels through the bush visiting each village, and if any man has received wrong at the hands of his neighbour he pays the Duk-duk so much dewarra to settle the question. This functionary then goes off to the aggressor's house, and demands restitution of the stolen goods, or payment for the harm done, which if the person accused does not pay, or restore at once, the Duk-duk sets fire to his house, or in some extreme cases spears the offender. Women and children are not allowed to look at the Duk-duk, or they will die. This superstition is so strong amongst them that they will run away and hide themselves as soon as they hear him coming, which they know by a peculiar shrieking noise he makes as he goes along.

When the young men are old enough they are admitted into the secret, on payment of about one hundred fathoms of dewarra, which if they cannot pay they must always keep out of his way.

At stated periods the Duk-duk goes his rounds, and afterwards there is a big feast and a dance, at which all the initiated attend ; and there is much dancing and dressing up in flowers and fern leaves on the occasion.

There is sometimes more than one Duk-duk if the chief can afford it ; no man is allowed to lift his hand against him, but must submit to everything the Duk-duk does, if not his life is not worth a day's purchase, as the chief of that Duk-duk's district will find a method of putting the offender quietly out of the way.

The secrets of the Duk-duk are not allowed to be spoken of outside the "taboo-ground," where he is supposed to live; and no one who is not initiated is allowed on that ground under a penalty of a heavy fine, or, if this be not paid, of death.

A case occurred at Rukukuroo where a young man was driven, through stress of weather, in his canoe on to the taboo-ground, and it happened that the Duk-duk was holding, or just about to hold, a feast. The young man was seized and carried to the Duk-duk who tomahawked him on the spot, and served his body as part of the feast in course of preparation.

Of course no one outside the Duk-duk Society ever knew what had become of the poor fellow.

The Duk-duk is both a curse and a blessing of his people; he certainly keeps order and makes the natives afraid to commit any flagrant act of felony, but at the same time it encourages cannibalism and terrorism.

There are secret signs between the initiated by which they know each other from outsiders. It is curious how widely distributed is this Duk-duk system in the north peninsula of New Britain; it is in nearly every district, also in New Ireland, from the west coast lying south of the Rossel Mountains to Cape St. George, and how far it may spread on the other side I cannot say.

Duke of York Island is the stronghold of the

system, and I fancy it originated there, though there are good arguments in favour of Birara. Tor Poulo says it began in Duke of York, but then he is chief of that place; and though he might know, he lives in that group, and I find these natives always inclined to boast about the place they live in (this is not only peculiar to savages!), therefore his statement must be taken *cum grano salis*.

The evidence in favour of Birara's being the original place in which the system started, is borne out by a legend told me by a very intelligent young man, who was himself a native of Duke of York, which strengthens my belief in his story.

He said: " A great many seasons ago (monsoons) there was a young man quarrelled with his father and all his family, and started off by himself into the bush. Having nothing to eat he became very hungry, and at last hit upon a plan to get flesh to eat.

" He made a large head-dress out of cane, and painted it with the juice of the betel-nut, and made eyes on it like the morroop's (cassowary's). He then dressed himself up in leaves so that his hands were hidden, and yet he could use them at pleasure, took a club and wandered off through the bush, making a noise as he went to frighten people.

" In this way he surprised many young boys and girls, whom he killed, and carried their bodies away to eat them.

" At last it got so bad, and every one was so terrified, that the father of the young man, who was a great fighting chief, determined to go out and conquer this monster.

"He overcame the Duk-duk in a struggle, and the latter was thrown to the ground; he then called out that he was the chief's son, and that if his father would spare him he would show him how to become powerful and get much dewarra.

"So the chief spared his life, and the monster that had frightened and killed so many became subject to his conqueror.

"He thenceforth lived by himself in a tabooed house, and every one was afraid to go near the place.

"If any one was rash enough to injure or disobey the chief, the Duk-duk would visit them with vengeance, and make them repent their temerity.

"The real secret of the people's terror rested in their not knowing what the Duk-duk was; they attributed superhuman powers to it, and this of course gave the Duk-duk great advantage, especially in the event of his having to fight. The women and children were ordered to keep out of the way, as it would probably kill them if it met them in the bush, and you may be sure they did not need telling twice.

"In course of time it was found necessary to let others into the secret; they were always admitted under an oath of secrecy, and so it spread from one place to another."

I think that the young native fully believed in the truth of this story, and allowing some latitude for the time that has occurred since the custom was started, it is very likely that something of the kind really did occur; but whether the site was Birara or Duke of York it is impossible to state.

It seems to remind one of the "Mumbo-Jumbo" of Africa; can it be possible that it is the remnant of a tradition brought from the original birthplace of these native tribes?

In speaking of the habits of the Duke of York natives and of the Duk-duk, one is reminded of the curious custom they have of propitiating the sea-god as it appears, though they do *not* in fact acknowledge any power of the water, and make out that the wind also is subservient to the wind-makers or doctors. Therefore I have reluctantly been obliged to put this curious and almost beautiful custom down to a piece of swindling on the part of the chief who inaugurates it, which is a great pity, as so much might have been made out of it about their worship.

One chief in each district (always the same man) has a canoe built (I do not think any special time of year is adhered to), and which is decorated with carved wood, flowers, ferns, and scented herbs.

It is then placed in a house by itself, which is of course tabooed, and no one may enter without paying so much dewarra, which they place in the canoe.

The chief (who is also a doctor) gives out that in order to catch plenty of fish this season every one must pay as much dewarra as possible into the canoe, that he (this chief) may make the fish easy to be caught.

This dewarra is supposed to be launched in the canoe to pay the fishes for those they lose by being caught; but the canoe is always carefully covered up when launched, and in reality not one shell of dewarra ever leaves the shore in that canoe, which floats away with the monsoon and is lost sight of.

If a bad season follows, of course the chief puts it down to there not being enough dewarra in the canoe; but not one native I have ever spoken to believes in it; that is, they do not believe it brings more fish; but they know it brings a feast and a dance, and they will do almost anything to obtain those.

So this custom, though still kept up, is not believed in now, however much faith may have been put in its efficacy formerly.

They have many dances in New Britain, and any excuse is sufficient for a "Malargen." The usual form of the dance is in two lines, like front and rear rank, and the dancers are dressed up in variegated leaves from the dracœna and other plants, and they have ferns and flowers on their heads and in their hands. The various kinds of dances are too numerous to describe, but, as I have said, they mostly consist of two lines of dancers, facing each other, who move their arms and legs in very correct time to the music, then turn either to the right or the left, and come round each other different ways.

I am afraid that short description is difficult to understand, but were I to attempt a fuller one I should get hopelessly confused.

There is one dance, however, I must try and describe—that is the " Toberran," which is arranged by the same chief that has the management of the fish canoe.

It occurs about once in two seasons at the full moon, and is really a very impressive sight; and the men and women who take part in it are all picked dancers.

At about nine P.M. we were all seated round in a large semicircle, the other side of the circle being formed by heaps of firewood, all ready for lighting. As yet there was no appearance of any performers, but by-and-by the tom-toms commenced to play very slowly, and the women, who were seated in front as orchestra, began to sing a weird kind of song, which I can only describe as a combined wailing of cats and dogs, which gradually got faster and faster. Presently one of the fires blazed up, and we saw some sort of creatures creeping out of the bush in all directions; they did indeed look like devils, which the word " Toberran " signifies. Some wore masks composed of skulls cut in half, and filled in with gum to represent a human face; these are held between the teeth by a stick, fastened across at the back of the mouth of the skull; on their heads they wore long black wigs composed of cocoa-nut fibre, and their bodies are covered with dead leaves.

Some that had no masks had their faces painted an unearthly green colour, and on their shoulders were fastened a kind of wings (on closer inspection I afterwards found these were actually fastened through the loose skin in the side of the neck).

On came these unearthly figures, creeping from the bush on every side, some with tails, some with spikes all down their backs, all keeping step and

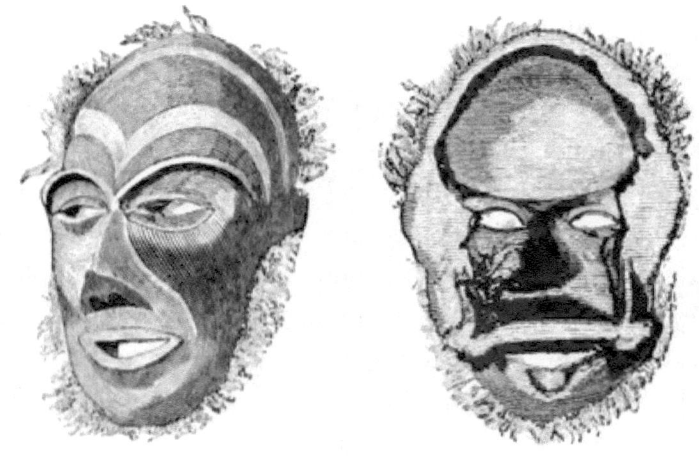

Front.   Back.

SKULL MASK, BLANCHE BAY, NEW BRITAIN.

beautiful time, no matter what position their bodies were in.

Suddenly the tom-toms stopped, and all the Toberrans rushed to the centre of the open space with a fearful yell ; then the music strikes up again, and there begins a dance that defies all description ; heads there, arms here, legs one way, tails another, and yet in perfect unison, for if there was an arm one side there was a leg to correspond on the other.

The shrieks and yells grew louder, and the singing became shouting; and as they dance, the fires are lighted and blaze up, throwing a lurid light on one of the most hideous scenes it has ever been my lot to witness.

Demon faces showing here, toothless skulls there,

TOM-TOM.

the air above them seeming full of arms smeared with blood, and below legs apparently in the last stages of mortification, and above all this a moon that sends a fitful light through the overhanging trees, whilst the huge fires alternately blazing up and dying down casting strange shadows which suggest things even more horrible than the frightful reality.

Indeed, however terribly we might try to put a "Dance of Death" on one of our stages, we could never equal this in its diabolical and hideous effects.

The tom-toms I mentioned, or drums, are hollow wooden cylinders, burnt out inside, in shape somewhat like two cones joined at the apex, covered at one end with iguana skin tightly stretched. This instrument is held under the arm or across the knee and is beaten with the hand.

There is also a larger drum called "garamoot," made of the trunk of a tree, hollowed out, I believe, by dropping small red-hot stones continually into the inside through a small slit on one side. The cylinder is struck with a long stick just below this slit, and produces a deep note that can be heard for an immense distance in calm weather.

Drums of this latter kind are heavy, and therefore are seldom moved from the dancing-ground, which is generally an open space in front of a chief's house, and is kept swept and clean by women specially appointed to look after it. The "garamoot" is also used for alarm signals in case of war, when it is struck so as to give a sharp quick sound, also for calling the people together.

There is another kind of drum, composed of three pieces of soft wood cut with a slight cavity on the under side of each; these are laid across the knees and beaten with two short sticks with heads to them, something like our small drum-sticks.

The other native musical instruments are a fife,

made from a small piece of bamboo, on which they can play three or four notes; pan-pipes, also made

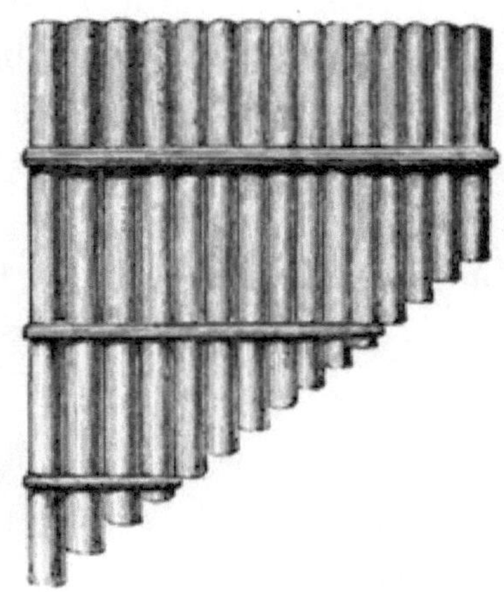

PAN PIPES, NEW BRITAIN.

of bamboo with seven pipes or more, and a jews' harp very cleverly constructed. It is a piece of bamboo

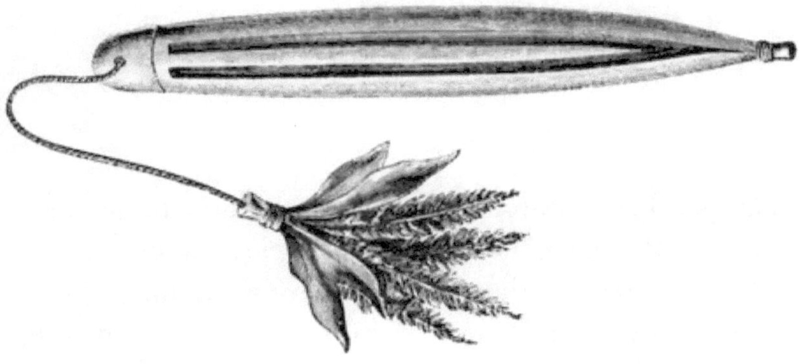

JEWS' HARP, NEW BRITAIN.

cut into a shape resembling a frond of the fern we call " hart's tongue," with a vibrator down the centre ; it is played resting against the mouth in the same

manner as our jews' harp is, except that the thumb
of the left hand is always used. There is also a piece
of string passed tightly over the instrument from
the thick end, which is struck against the vibrator.

Another small instrument looks like a primitive
banjo; this consists of a large piece of bamboo, cut
through at the joint horizontally and also about four
inches above the joint, another small flat piece of

INSTRUMENT OF MUSIC.

bamboo being fastened across the mouth, projecting
beyond the edge of the circular piece about three
inches; thus very much resembling a banjo. There
are, however, only two strings made of a piece of the
outer bark of a cane that grows in these islands;
these are stretched tightly along the projecting piece
of bamboo, and fastened below on to the larger
portion by a wooden peg.

It is played with a small stick, struck sharply

against the strings, making two humming notes. These instruments appear to be common to all these islands, and are to be seen in any village, and in almost every home, except the larger drums which belong especially to the chiefs.

The ornaments of the Duke of York natives are fewer and less used than in either New Britain or New Ireland; they consist chiefly of dewarra shells formed into necklets or placed round the head. The ear-lobes are cut, and distended by inserting rolled leaves of a springy nature, generally pandannas leaves, which, constantly pressing against the sides of the opening, enlarge it till in some cases it hangs nearly to the shoulder. The nose is also pierced on each side of the nostrils, and a small sharp-pointed piece of wood inserted in each hole ; on the wood are sometimes threaded a few beads (when they have them) ; more commonly there is only the wood, which I was informed is to act as a "sight" for throwing the spears, though I can scarcely think it would help an European to do anything else but squint.

Variegated leaves are tucked under the armlet, which is made of plaited twine and dyed with different coloured juices. These armlets are worn so tight that they squeeze the arm out of shape, and in many cases cannot be got off except by cutting them through ; if not so tight as this, however, they may be moved by oiling and pressing the arm.

The men of the island of Duke of York, and indeed throughout the whole group, wear no clothes ;

but the women of Mioko, Utuan, and the South Peninsula wear a small covering hanging in front and behind, made of grass dyed bright red.

These natives fish with a rod, the hook being of tortoise-shell, but they more often prefer going on to the reefs with a small narrow net, which they spread out with stakes, and then drive the fish into it, where they become meshed.

They have also a net stretched on poles something like a shrimping net, with which they catch the shoals of small fish that at certain seasons visit these shores in great numbers, and are delicious eating.

It is a curious and remarkable fact that there are no cassowaries or white cockatoos to be found on Duke of York Island, although in New Britain there are a great many of the former birds and thousands of the latter.

The only cockatoos in Duke of York are those that have been brought over from New Britain, to which place they always return if they make their escape.

I cannot discover any reason for this peculiar fact, as there appears to be much the same kind of feed for these birds on one island as on the other. The cassowaries may all have been killed off Duke of York Island, as it is more thickly populated than New Britain; but were this the case one would expect to find them on New Ireland, but they are not to be found there either.

Duke of York Island is only fourteen or fifteen miles from New Britain at the furthest, and New Ireland only thirty or so, a distance that could easily be traversed by the cockatoos. I can therefore see no accountable reason for their non-existence.

The fruits on Duke of York Island consist of the banana, cocoa-nut, tan, mummy-apple, and a kind of wild mango. Yams and taro also grow on the island, but sweet potatoes are the chief product, and serve as one of the main articles of trade between this and the other islands.

The bananas in some parts of Duke of York are very fine, but the yams and taro are not to be compared with those of New Britain, or the yams of New Ireland, which are noted for their size; the taro of New Britain is considered the finest in the South Seas.

Perhaps all my readers do not know what taro is; I will therefore try and describe it. It is a large bulbous tuber, with leaves of much the same shape as the caladium, but I have never seen it in flower.

There are two different kinds, one of which grows in swampy ground, the other on the hillside, the latter being the largest and the best, as the swamp taro is waxy to eat. It is planted in rows about one pace apart, and kept clear of weeds by the women. The hill taro grows to the size of fifteen inches long by twelve inches in circumference, that is considered a large one.

When cooked in only a small quantity of water, the starch that exudes from it makes the water into a thick paste, it therefore requires water to be added continually; when cooked it is soft and mealy, and one of the best vegetables I have ever eaten.

The native way of preparing it is even better than boiling it; they first scrape off the rough outside brown coating with a sharp shell, and after cutting the taro in half lengthways, wrap it in banana leaves and place it in a fire where it is not too hot. When cooked it is very much like good new bread, and is extremely nutritious. After taking the taro out of the ground, the tuber is cut off, leaving about one inch of it still adhering to the stalk and leaves; this is replanted, and in about three months another large tuber is ready for cutting.

The leaves are very astringent, and if eaten raw will take the skin off the mouth, and render it very sore for some days; but the young leaves cooked with cocoa-nut milk make a very delicious dish.

Tan is a fruit which I do not suppose many Europeans know anything about. It grows on very high trees, whose wood, by the way, is beautifully grained and very hard, though at the same time nice to work. The fruit is shaped like an apple, and grows in bunches as some apples do; but when ripe, if you take one in your hand and press it, the skin will come off entirely, and the inside is a beautiful clear, jelly-like substance that melts into water in your mouth.

This jelly surrounds a brown stone, of which the natives make a sort of cake, after it has been soaked for some days in salt water.

The papaw, or mummy-apple, has also some curious facts connected with it, which are useful to know. The young fruit, when boiled, makes a delicious substitute for vegetable marrow; whilst the stalks and leaves, if boiled with clothes, will make them beautifully clean and white; the clothes come out of the boiler a bright gamboge-yellow, but when hung up in the air to dry, they turn perfectly white again. Also a small piece of the leaf or stalk boiled with an old fowl or a tough piece of meat will make it quite tender.

CHAPTER IV.

NEW BRITAIN—KININIGUNUN.

WE sailed from Duke of York for Kininigunun, in order that I might build a house, which was to serve as a depôt for inland work. The first difficulty was to decide in which part of this district to build, for Kininigunun is a large one, and extends in a W.N.W. direction from Gazelle Point to Rulunana Point. It contains smaller districts within it, of which Abercole is at the S.E. and Rulunana at the N.W. ends, whilst the centre is Kininig-u-nun proper, and it was here that I at last settled to build.

I was greatly indebted to one of Mr. Brown's Fijian teachers for his assistance; he worked for me splendidly. I soon made arrangements with Tor-Rarrabay, one of the chiefs, for the purchase of a very fine piece of land on the coast, close down to the water in front, but extending a considerable way into the bush at the back, and beyond again to a small open plain covered with long grass, near which lay one of the main tracks inland.

My house was a large one, sixty feet long by twenty feet broad, and a good height; it was of native material and roofed with long grass.

It was divided into four rooms, two sleeping-rooms, a cupboard, and the rest for a general room. At the back was the cooking-house and garden, the whole being enclosed with a double fence of bamboo.

The natives were friendly and seemed anxious to please, each one helping a little all round, though they made a great noise over it; indeed, they seem unable to do anything without making a great deal of noise.

When everything was finished, we had a big feast and a dance by way of house-warming; Tor-Rarra-bay asked me if *he* should provide a human body for the feast, upon which I told him in the strongest terms I could command, never even to *think* of such a thing again, as white men hated cannibalism, and that I could not bear to think of him as one.

After this I never heard it mentioned again, so pigs, yams, taro, bananas, &c., in profusion formed our feast; and after the dancing, I served out tobacco and pipes all round.

Our first journey inland was in order to see a battle between the Kininigunun tribe and another from the interior.

We went through the bush for about two or three miles, amongst high trees and thick scrub, after which we came upon more open ground, with banana plantations, and here my guides began to move more cautiously, as we were approaching the fighting-ground.

Presently we heard the shouting of the combatants, and coming out into an open plain, found the natives hard at work with their slings.

It was apparently only a skirmish, as the main body of the opposing tribe were quite half a mile off, and only a few on each side were actually engaged.

These slings they use are composed of oblong pieces of bark, with two strings of about a yard in length fastened to either end, on one of which is a button of pearl-shell, in order that the sling may not slip through their fingers. The stone rests in the centre, on the oblong piece of bark.

They use these slings with great accuracy and considerable force; indeed, I have seen a native discharge a stone to the distance of two hundred and fifty yards with sufficient force to break it against another; but I believe it is more knack than strength that is required to use them.

The natives engaged were running about in the long grass, and dodging to escape the stones from the enemies' side.

As we were on high ground near the Kininigunun tribe, we could see all that was going on, and observed that the natives who were fighting had only their slings. This, I presume, was in order that they might move more freely, and as they seldom come close to the enemy, other weapons would have been useless.

Whilst I was watching, Tor-Rarrabay (who, by the way, is considered a great warrior) came up to me and entreated me to go away, for fear I should get hurt. As I could not see the smallest chance of it, I told him that I was not more likely to get hurt than he was, and that the white man never ran away because there was fighting going on. He then informed me that they were only waiting for one of the other side to be hit with a stone, to attack with the whole force (and the other side the same, I presume).

Soon after he left me; I suppose this must have happened, as a great shouting was raised by the Kininigunun tribe, they beginning at the same time the "too-tooing" noise they make when anything exciting occurs, and a general rush forward of the whole body was made to join the skirmishers, women following with bundles of spears and stones for the slings.

However, there was not much fighting done, as the other side took to their heels and ran for the bush. I heard afterwards that the conquerors obtained two bodies, which of course were eaten, though they took good care not to let me know *where,* yet I heard it from a " private source," as we say.

Tor-Rarrabay was very boastful when I met him afterwards about winning the battle, but I dashed his ardour somewhat by saying, "if he called *that* fighting I did not think much of it." I then told him about the white men's fighting ; upon which he asked me what was done with all the bodies, hoping evidently to make me confess that they were eaten ; but when I told him they were buried, he turned away, evidently in disgust at such a waste.

The war had been about some houses on the plain, which had been burnt, the men murdered, and the women carried off. It terminated in a tragedy which occurred soon after the battle. Some young men of the bush tribe came into Kininigunun district to see if they could not pick up a stray man or woman.

Instead of this they were themselves surrounded, and being young and active, fought hard for their lives, but were overpowered by numbers. A few of them were taken alive ; these of course were tortured, one manner being to tie the victim's hands and feet to stakes in the ground, and place fire on his stomach. This fiendish operation is done by the women, who are far more cruel than the men, as a man will some-times free the poor wretch from his pain by a spear thrust, or a blow from a tomahawk, but the women will laugh at and enjoy it, poking the sufferer with a spear to rouse him up if he do not writhe and howl enough to satisfy them.

The women generally accompany their husbands to war, carrying their spears, stones, &c., and excite them by their language ; but as the women are looked upon as little more than beasts of burden by the men, how can one expect anything better ?

One of the chief's spies told me that if he wished

to find anything particular he always listened behind a tree to the women talking, and he was sure to find out all he wished to know.

They have a saying in New Britain, " Never trust any secret to a woman, for their tongues are hung with a double joint."

Here it may be well to give some account of a woman's social position.

When a man intends to take a wife he tells his father who it is (if he has no father he tells his mother or the chief of the district).   He then is sent off into the bush, where he stays for some days, until the father calls him back; the father and mother in the meantime go to the girl's relations, and after making them presents say they will pay so much dewarra for the girl.

There is a great deal of haggling over the price, and the girl's relations generally succeed in raising it; when settled, the man's father and mother go home again.   On the day fixed the young woman's relations go to the house of the man's father and mother, who have (if rich enough) invited all their friends to meet them ; the former give presents to their host and there is a feast and a dance ; also a young women's dance, in which the bride-elect is supposed to take a leading part.

After all this festivity is over, the girl is left with the young man's parents, and he is called in from the bush, that is to say, some one is sent to find him, which is sometimes a difficult matter, as these young men often go a long way, in order to escape from the spirits of departed relations, who are said to exercise a very bad influence at this time.

It is not an uncommon thing for the young man never to return, having been killed by some hostile tribe.

Marriages are often settled before the woman is born; for instance, should a chief wish to marry into any particular family, he buys the child when there is a prospect of one being born. Should it be a boy, the "taboo" is returned, but if a girl the "taboo" is retained by her family, and the girl becomes the property, and ultimately the wife, of the chief, though she lives with her parents until a marriageable age—about ten years.

The woman at her marriage becomes completely the property of the man, even to power over her life, as for instance, a chief who lives on the shore of Blanche Bay had purchased a young wife, who cried and wished to go back to her friends, and would do no work. Upon this her husband became angry, and telling her that as she was no use as a wife he would make use of her in another way, which he did by immediately killing her and cooking her body for a feast.

There was also a case here in Kininigunun, where a man belonging to a bush tribe was surprised in the bush with his wife, and taken prisoner by one of the sub-chiefs and a few followers. They killed the man, but the woman was taken to be one of the sub-chief's wives; and the marriage-feast was the body of her late husband.

The laws against intermarriage are very strict : there are in every tribe two distinct parties between whom *only* is marriage allowed; generally the men buy women from foreign tribes, having found, no doubt, as we have done, that intermarriage weakens the race.

The chief of the tribe must be asked for his permission before marriage can be contracted. Should a young man who is unable to purchase a wife be desirous of doing so, he goes to his chief and asks him to buy one for him. If the chief knows that the young man is likely to be able to pay him back either in dewarra, work, or fighting, he will purchase the wife for him, and also make a feast on the occasion, but the chiefs are careful to see first that there is a likelihood of their being repaid in some way.

The women carry their babies in net-work bags, the band or strap of which comes round the forehead, and the child in the bag rests on their shoulder-blades, and in travelling to market or elsewhere, should the child require suckling, they do it over the shoulder.

They will also carry two or three cocoa-nut mat bags full of merchandise on their back, as well as the baby; this gives them a stooping gait, and makes them always walk in a double-up manner, even when not carrying anything.

Women also suffer from the skin disease " Buck-war " in common with the men; it appears to turn the skin a lighter colour than when it is healthy.

My second long journey inland was taken with the intention of reaching Mount Beautemps Beaupré, which is situated about thirty miles from the coast, and is a high volcanic peak of about one thousand eight hundred feet, and would have been a grand place for observation on the contour of the surrounding country.

Having obtained as guides Tor-Rarrabay and several other natives, we made all preparations for staying away four days. Tor-Rarrabay told me he had never been so far inland, but boasted he was not afraid to go anywhere.

So we set off, going along the tracks in Indian file, I myself bringing up the rear.

In front of me was a young man carrying my observing instruments and ammunition, next to him came Tor-Rarrabay in full dress, with spear and tomahawk, in front of him other natives with provisions, &c., and the guides leading the way.

We took a general course of S.W. by W., which brought us to a more northerly part of the plain, on which the fight I have previously described took place.

I here noticed a most peculiar feature of the land, namely, a natural wall, composed mostly of decayed pumice-stone, which rose about twelve feet from the level on which we stood. It appeared as though the land where we were standing must have suddenly sunk and left this wall, which extended for several miles.

The land on the other side was level with the top

of the wall, but on ours it was perpendicular, cut as smoothly as if by the hand of man.

The natives did not seem to recognise it as anything strange, but then they have no knowledge of other lands, and can only know of what is in their own small range of travel.

After passing over the plain, which was in some places covered with high grass, and in others was bare, where the grass had been burnt away, we again entered a thin belt of dense scrub, so thick in some places that we were obliged to cut our way with tomahawks and knives.

This extended for half-a-mile, when we again emerged on to a beautiful grassy table-land. We were now about six hundred feet above the sea, which was just visible in the distance, with New Ireland showing far beyond.

We had come about twelve miles, and decided to camp a little further on, where there was fresh water, and a slight scrub for firewood. It appeared to me whilst in conversation with Tor-Rarrabay that he did not appear quite so brave and boastful about getting to the mountain as he had done when we started, for he began to tell me all the stories he could think of about " devils " in that part of the country, and how people who had gone towards the mountain had never returned, &c., &c. !

However, I determined not to take any notice, and answered, " Oh, yes, but *we* are not afraid to go anywhere." This seemed to remind him of his talk in

Kininigunun, and he replied, "Oh, no," though somewhat doubtfully.

Next morning we started off again towards a village belonging to a tribe at peace with Tor-Rarrabay. We kept on over the grassy tableland, that seemed to extend on both sides as far as I could see, until about eight o'clock A.M.; we then came to the village, which was prettily situated on a rising knoll and surrounded with cocoa-nut trees.

We stopped in the open place in front of the chief's house, and received a very hearty welcome from him; he was an elderly man of about fifty, I should say.

Tor-Rarrabay introduced me with a great flourish, and explained that I was living with him—a little stroke of policy on his part, meant to show that he was powerful enough to have a white man living in his village. He told this chief of a hundred different qualities of mine, of which had I possessed but the half I should have been far away the cleverest man in the world; of course this was one for me and half-a-dozen for himself.

The chief of "Nucgunigu," as this place appeared to be called, was determined to display his hospitality to the new arrivals, and so our coming was the occasion of a murder so horrible that I can never get the sight of it out of my mind. After the betel-nut had been duly discussed, our host said something to Tor-Rarrabay that I could not understand, and the old villain must have given his consent, or this would never have occurred whilst I was there, at all events.

Presently I saw two men lead forward another man who had his hands tied behind him.

Never having seen anything of the kind before, I did not in the least know what was going to happen. They led the prisoner up to the chief, and made him sit down in front of him, and they all looked so pleasant and friendly one would never have suspected anything fearful was going to take place. The prisoner had his back to a dead tree, which I noticed was painted in red and white stripes, and had a number of pigs' jawbones hung about it ; it also had a kind of signal halyards, made of cane, suspended from the topmost branch ; this was presently taken round and made fast to the other side of the tree. The chief now began to ask the man questions, some of which I could understand, such as : " Have you any father and mother ? " Then followed others ; and then, " Will you eat or drink ? " was the last I understood.

Upon this a woman brought him a cocoa-nut, which she held to his mouth whilst he drank from it.

I asked Tor-Rarrabay what was going to happen, but all he would say was, " You will see." Presently some young men went to the back of the tree, and one of them, quick as lightning, slipped the end of a noose round the prisoner's neck, and the men behind the tree began to hoist.

I knew that Tor-Rarrabay was watching me very closely to see the effect it had upon me, so it behove me to be very careful.

"Tell the chief," said I, "that if he will sell me that man alive I will give him six tomahawks and as much red cloth and beads as one man can carry.' But Tor-Rarrabay answered, "What is the use? I will sell you a man for that, and you would only offend this chief, and—we are on his ground"—a very significant hint, as there must have been about three hundred or more people there.

The sight was now sickening, as the poor fellow was hanging with his toes just reaching the ground; so that he was being gradually choked to death, and at the same time a number of women rushed at him, and began beating him with their hands and with stones on the stomach. It was a fearful sight; I had a deadly feeling, yet I dared not show any repugnance.

"Ask the chief to let me show him how *white men* kill men with their guns," I said to Tor-Rarrabay, with as much unconcern in my voice as I could muster. "No, no!" said Tor-Rarrabay, "no one would eat him after if you shot him, for fear he was poisoned."

How truly thankful I was when the poor victim's sufferings were terminated by a man who only waited a sign from the chief to thrust a knife slowly into the sufferer's heart, and with one convulsive struggle all was over. I *tried* to make myself believe it was a bullock they were cutting up afterwards.

At the feast I told Tor-Rarrabay that I was "tabooed" from eating any flesh whilst on this journey, which saved me from taking *any* meat. I managed a little fruit, but even that was hard work after what I had seen.

Some people may say I might have interfered more than I did ; but all I can say is, one cannot be *too* careful not to offend, when it is such tremendous odds as *one* against three or four hundred ; and though fire-arms and an Englishman may do wonders, yet it would have been too great a risk, and I did the best thing I could, which was first to try and buy the man, that could not offend any one ; but being refused, next to try and put him quickly out of pain. But when denied that request, there was no more to be done.

Whilst we are on this subject, and it is one that cannot be avoided if New Britain is to be described, we may as well go through with it at once.

Each chief has two ministers, or dependents, a talking man, and a butcher. These are permanent : the former does all the talking, the latter the killing and cutting up. The part of a man that sells for most "taboo" is the thigh, that of a woman the breast ; the head is never eaten, nor are the entrails, they are buried. The leg and arm bones of men who are enemies are placed at the butt end of spears, as the natives believe it gives them the strength of the man whose bone they carry. They also think that it makes them invulnerable to any wounds from the eaten man's relations. They seldom eat a man of their own tribe ; but should one have been killed by his own chief, or a member of the tribe for wrong doing, the body may be sold to another tribe; women are more often killed and eaten by their own friends!

I have said all I need to say I hate to write about such things, more even than you do to read of them, for I have seen and remember the sight only too well.

At about four P.M. we had to start again on our journey, of which I was very glad. Tor-Rarrabay could, I feel sure, have stopped that horrible spectacle if he had chosen; but I think he wanted to see what I should do, and to frighten me, if possible, into going back, as I know now that he himself was afraid to go much further inland.

We travelled on, still over plain-land, but it was now more rocky, and covered in places with stunted bushes, with not much cultivation to be seen. Mount Beautemps Beaupré towering up above us so close, it appeared as if we should be there in half-an-hour. I knew, however, it was still some miles off, and the sun was going down.

As we went along Tor-Rarrabay kept on hinting that the men would not go any further, as the other chief had told them there were very bad spirits living in these parts, and they were afraid; he thought it would be better for us to return.

However, I succeeded in getting them along till it was time to camp, by promises of large presents, and inventing all manner of yarns as to how I could overcome any evil spirit because I was more power-ful than they were. I fear, though, I did not convince them.　As the sun went down we camped; fortunately we had brought water with us this last stage, as there did not appear to be any in the neighbourhood, and it proved a wise step.

After supper we lay down, but it was a long time before I could sleep; and instead began to think of our journey.　Here we were only five miles from the base of the mountain, a short valley to cross, and we could begin the ascent, which would not be a difficult one.　Then, after taking bearings and sights, we might return, and I should have accomplished the object of my journey, and found out many things I wished to know.

Next I began to think of dear old England and my home, and wondered if they could see me now what they would think, till at last I fell asleep.

Next morning the sun was not yet risen, when I suddenly woke, and jumped up with that indescribable feeling that tells you you are alone.　Yes! too true, after I had fallen asleep, or very early in the morning, Tor-Rarrabay and all the guides had decamped, and, what was worse, all the provisions and water were gone with them, as well as the ammunition, save about ten rounds of small shot cartridges for my fowling-piece, and five charges in my revolver.　I did not at once take in my situation, for I had made up my mind to go on, and on, and climb the mountain.　But then I thought, "I do not know what sort of people are on that mountain, and also, I shall be going further away from where I can get food and water, for should I meet any natives on the mountain, they will surely take me for a devil, and run away from me, even if they do nothing worse. Anyhow, I cannot reckon upon getting provisions from them, and I have not ammunition enough to force my way up; besides, if I did so, it would interfere with my getting up in a friendly way, should I be so fortunate as ever to get here another time. So I must go back, but not by that horrible village."

Thus reasoning, I determined to start, and rejoiced to find my little prismatic compass in my pocket, and made up my mind to steer a straight line for Blanche Bay, as this would be the most open country and the shortest way.

I knew I had nothing to fear from the natives as soon as I was in Ruluanna district, and, moreover, by taking this line of country I should avoid Nuegunigu, where I should have been either murdered straight off, or kept to make " things grow."

The idea amongst these natives with respect to the trade articles the white men bring is that they are all grown just as they are—tomahawks, beads, knives, redcloth, looking-glasses, all grow, and therefore we must have an unlimited supply.

This, I imagine, is because they have nothing of their own that does not grow, except the stone for their tomahawks, and this is found in the country. Then had these people found I could not make the things they wished for grow, I should have been put out of the way.

These may have been foolish ideas of mine, and no

doubt were, still it was not strange that I should feel suspicious after what I had seen there the day before, and I do not think my nerves were very steady, or perhaps I should have acted differently. However, I started off and pushed through the long grass as fast as I could.

On my way over the plains I saw many flocks of cassowaries, and once or twice a wallaby springing along over the cleared burnt patches, or stopping to nibble at the fresh green blades that were forcing their way up through the blackened vegetation above.

I will now leave myself struggling through the long grass and try to explain what these large burnt patches of grass mean. No doubt, they are sometimes the result of carelessness on the part of the natives, but are perhaps more often the results of the method they adopt to catch the wild pigs and the cassowaries which abound on these plains. On the day fixed for the sport they send out the women and boys early in the day, who on reaching the appointed spot spread themselves out into a large circle or cordon of perhaps a mile in circumference, or even more, according to their numbers.

At a given signal, which is generally a smoke from the bush-grass, fired at one place, they all light the grass by them, and along to where the next person has lighted theirs, forming a wide circle of fire, which on the outside edge is well beaten down, to prevent its spreading *too* far.

One opening is left to windward ; towards this all

the frightened animals within the circle rush, and are speared as they come out. Large numbers are taken in this way; sometimes when a tribe has killed more than enough for themselves the chief sends all that is not wanted as presents to the surrounding friendly chiefs.

As I went along (keeping my course as well as I could, for the long grass and clumps of trees) I saw in the distance what appeared a good-sized freshwater lake on the N.E. side of Mount Beautemps Beaupré—it had a small island in the centre. I could not see any river falling into, or flowing out from it, so it may be of the same formation as the water-hole that lies in the crater of the Mother Mountain, which also has apparently no outlet or inflow, and which I sounded to the depth of five hundred fathoms, no bottom. Yet it has fish in it: the only other instance I know of this is at Pantelleria, an island in the Mediterranean off the N. coast of Africa.

After travelling on some distance further, I began to feel the want of water very much, and also was getting exhausted for want of food. I had seen nothing of any natives, or I might have been tempted to force them to give me water, but while I was considering what was best to do, I suddenly bethought me of some betel-nut and lime which I had in my pocket. This I at once began to chew, and found that it entirely satisfied both thirst and hunger. This nut is eaten with the flower or catkin of the pepper-plant, or with the leaves; these are dipped in powdered burnt lime. It turns the saliva quite red, and tends to make the teeth black. It was an immense relief to have found I had it.

Night was now coming on, and I determined to lie down in the long grass and have a good sleep if possible, in order to be fresher for going on next morning early. However, I found it impossible to sleep, and every rustle of the grass seemed to me to be natives creeping upon me. There was only a faint reflection of light in the horizon, when I was up and off again. I was in great hopes of reaching Ruluanna that day, but was hardly calculating upon the very hard work it is to struggle through the thick grass and still denser bush; and having no boots, my feet were getting very sore.

I found boots were too hot and heavy for travelling in; besides, all mine were worn out. If ever I should have to do this sort of work again I certainly will lay in a good stock of moccasins. On I went, still chewing my betel-nut and pushing my way through the grass, though the sharp stubble was very painful to tread upon. About midday I saw a thick belt of trees ahead which gave me fresh hope and spirits, as I could shelter there from the fierce sun. which was literally baking my brain. Indeed, I fancy I must have been somewhat delirious, for I found myself (I don't know how) rolling on the ground in the shade of the trees, as if I had been in water. I was soon off again, however, pushing through the scrub, and having my clothes torn in the most ill-natured way by the prickly palms.

I began now to suffer very much from the want of water, though the betel-nut continued to soothe my mouth somewhat, causing saliva to flow, yet I found in my exhausted state I could hardly stand the very mild intoxicating effect it has. A small piece of tobacco that I tried to chew seemed to burn my mouth like fire. As night came on again I seemed possessed with a sort of fierce determination to get on at all risks. When about sundown I fell into a native track. Oh! what a relief was that smooth ground to walk upon, and an assurance of its leading *somewhere!* I did not care where now, for I was getting desperate, and I could not have gone more than a mile-and-a-half when I came to a water-hole.

I flung myself down, and drank—well, I suppose I did not empty the pool; but I felt as though I could have done so. Then I lay down by it, and fell asleep, regardless of all dangers. Luckily no natives came whilst I was there. It was about eight A.M. before I woke, refreshed but very weak; however, I judged I could not now be more than ten miles from the outskirts of Ruluanna. The travelling, too, was comparatively easy, and I got along pretty well.

Soon I began to come upon signs of natives, by finding patches cleared for yams, &c., and at midday met some native women carrying their heavy loads to market.

I stopped them and bought some cocoa-nuts with a few beads I had left, and sitting down there and then ate a whole one, much to the astonishment of the women, who were startled at seeing a white man at all, to say nothing of finding him so far in the bush. After the cocoa-nut I felt much stronger and got on quite quickly; soon I saw native houses, then native men, who at first appeared suspicious as to what I might want there, but I reassured them, and they took me down to the chief's house. Here I was given some yams and cooked taro, and I thought it was the most delicious food I had ever eaten. I got the loan of a canoe from this chief, and after walking about half-a-mile came to the beach, and embarked for Kininigunun, which lies to the east further along the coast.

On arriving at Kininigunun, I found Tor-Rarrabay had not been seen on board the vessel, or at my house, yet when I went ashore I found that every-thing my guides had carried off when they left me was put back again into the house. So I sent up word to Tor-Rarrabay to come and see me, and not to be afraid. By-and-by he came, and told me the reason they ran away was, because one of the men declared he had seen a "toberran," or evil spirit, and that the others were all frightened. *He* was not; he only went with them in case they might get into trouble with other tribes. You can imagine how much of this story I believed.

He seemed greatly astonished to see me again, as he evidently thought I could never find my way back without a guide. "Oh," said I, "I had a guide," and showed him my compass, which he regarded with mysterious awe, and would scarcely touch. " Yes," I said, " that was my guide, and a better one than you and your men, for it did not run away and leave me alone."

CHAPTER V.

WE had made arrangements with Mr. Brown, the Wesleyan missionary whom I have already introduced, to go with him along the coast to Spacious Bay, he bringing his little steam-launch to do the inshore work; so we left Kininigunun for Duke of York. from which place we were to start. Shortly before this I had lost poor Bluff: the poor thing had jumped overboard to swim ashore after the boat in which I was, when we saw a crocodile seize her and drag her under, and we never saw her again.

We crossed to Duke of York, and found Mr. Brown all ready for our journey, with steam up in his launch; and on the 1st of January, 1878, we started for Spacious Bay.

We sailed and steamed down St. George's Channel, crossing to New Britain to the south of Duke of York group, and fetched Gazelle Point (Birara).

From this place we ran along the coast to a small bay, in which was an island and a sandbank with a large river running into it at the southern end.

There was also a small barrier reef on the outer and north side of the bay. We did not see any natives, and the only sign of them was the presence of a good many turtle bones, which must have been cooked there by them. From this bay the land trends somewhat to the south and east, until Cape Palliser is reached, when the line of the coast takes a south-west direction to Cape Buller, which cape forms the north headland of Spacious Bay. This part of the coast is hilly, pretty steep hills too, and is thickly covered with bush. From Cape Buller the coast falls more to the south, and is intersected with small bays and creeks, until Archway Point is reached, so called from its being a curious natural archway with a span of about twenty yards straight out into the sea. It is covered with ferns and creepers, and there is a depth of three fathoms immediately beneath the arch, it being high enough to allow a good-sized vessel to pass underneath. On the outside it is precipitous; on the south-west side is a small embayment, in which we anchored for the night.

There was a small freshwater creek at the north end of this bay, and whilst we were there some natives came down. I went on shore to try and converse with them, but found their language was quite different from that spoken either in Birara or Kininigunun. These natives had also apparently never *seen* white men before, though they must have heard of them, for though they were very frightened they did not run away. I went ashore by myself, in the "dingy," in order not to frighten them away.

There happened to be a cocoa-nut in the boat, which they immediately made signs for; I therefore think that in this district there can be no cocoa-nut palms, though probably they buy them from adjoining tribes. These natives wear a waist-cloth, with a plaited tail hanging down behind, otherwise their arms and appearance are similar to those of the northern tribes.

After leaving Archway Point, we constantly observed natives along the shore, but were unable to hold any communication with them, owing to their assuming an exceedingly hostile appearance on our attempting to land, using the most objectionable gestures, apparently in order to show their contempt of us. Indeed, in one place where we were anchored in a small cove, they came down in great numbers on to the beach, and began to throw stones from their slings, so that it was considered advisable to haul further off the shore. The next headland is a long hilly point which stretches about three miles to the southward due south, and which I named Tongue Point from its shape. After leaving this point we found ourselves entering a most beautiful bay, which I named " Henry Reid " Bay, after the name of the missionary steam-launch.

The bay forms a complete harbour, measuring from Tongue Point to the W. shore four-and-a-half miles, with a stretch of about the same extent N. and S.

It is surrounded by a beautifully wooded shore; and on the N.W. side two rivers of considerable extent enter it, the northern and smaller one called

Pleasant River; the mouth of the one to the southward, about a mile distant from the former, is large and deep. At the entrance we found a depth of from two-and-a-half to three fathoms, which depth continued up the river for about half-a-mile, and we found sufficient water up the river for the steam-launch for about three miles. The course is in a westerly direction, trending slightly northwards.

At this distance up the river we landed on the north bank, and, going about two hundred yards into the bush, discovered a deserted fishing village of about twelve or thirteen huts, outside which were lying numbers of empty shells of river clam, which the natives seem to have been fishing for here, and probably the object that attracted them to this spot. The huts appeared to be newly constructed and could not long have been deserted, though they were so slightly built that I do not think the natives could have resided in them for any length of time.

The banks of the river were beautifully covered with ferns, intermingled with the sago and betel-nut palms. We observed, too, a beautiful creeper hanging from the trees with a magnificent red wax-like flower, also a kind of gum-tree (Eucalyptus), and some of the most lovely kinds of dracœnas lent their colours to enhance the general beauty of the scene. We found the water of the river was perfectly fresh at a quarter-of-a-mile from the mouth, and returned to the open water without seeing any signs of natives. Getting out into the bay again, we proceeded on our course towards Turner Point, which is the S. point of Henry Reid Bay, observing on the way a small island, lying close in to the S. shore also, about one-and-a-half to the northward, a small reef, on which there was a considerable break. Henry Reid Bay averages for the most part a depth of about twenty fathoms, though it shallows considerably towards the S. shore.

Whilst anchored in the bay we observed several large hornbills flying about amongst the trees, making that curious rushing noise with their wings like a railway train in motion, which obtains for them the native name of " Banga-banga." We also observed the foot-tracks of cassowaries on the shore, and one evening we saw a small wallaby come down to the beach, apparently to lick salt off the stones.

After rounding Turner Point we came upon a long stretch of low land, the beach running very nearly north and south for a distance of about four miles; upon it we observed a large number of natives, who were waving green branches, and gesticulating to us. After we had anchored, Mr. Brown and I determined to go ashore, though, having been so badly received hitherto, we were rather doubtful of the result. On landing the natives at first appeared to be rather shy of us, but after some little persuasion, and showing them strings of beads and red cloth, they began to venture round us; whereupon we began to barter for some small things they were wearing, such as armlets, necklets, &c. The first man who obtained a few beads appeared to be so much overcome by his immense wealth (as soon as he had them in his hands) that he rushed off along the beach yelling like a maniac, presumably to show his friends the wonderful treasure he had obtained from the mysterious creatures who had come to visit them. After this others were more eager to obtain a similar treasure, and pressed round us, trying to barter everything they had on, even the very rings out of their ears.

Wishing to purchase a pig, and not knowing very well how to set about it, as I was ignorant of the dialect, which is totally different from that spoken in the north, I asked Mr. Brown what would be the best way of making them understand. "Why don't you try grunting?" he said, whereupon I began to grunt most vociferously. The effect was magical— some of them jumped back, holding their spears in readiness to throw; some ran away, covering their eyes with their hands, and all exhibited the utmost astonishment and alarm; in fact, it was so evident that they expected me to turn into a pig, and their alarm was so irresistibly comic, that Mr. Brown and I both burst out laughing, which gradually reassured them, and those who had run away came back.

Seeing us so heartily amused, and that I had not undergone any metamorphosis, they began to laugh too, and upon my drawing a pig on the sand with a piece of stick, and making motions of eating, it suddenly seemed to strike them what was wanted, for they all burst out laughing again, and nodding their heads, several natives ran off, evidently in quest of the pig we required.

After this they were very much more friendly, and took us off to show us a village close by. When we got near, it struck me at once, seeing no women or children about, it must be a village they had conquered; and this idea as we came closer was confirmed by large heaps of human bones lying about, all charred and blackened by fire. I picked up what appeared to be a shin-bone, and showed it to a native with an inquiring look, whereupon he snatched it out of my hand, and, pointing to his own leg, put the bone into his mouth, and began munching all round it, at the same time rubbing his stomach, and grinning as much as to say it was very good. Although there were so many bones about, I did not see any skulls, which led me to imagine that they had been taken away for trophies. There was no appearance of any one living in the houses of this conquered village, and that was because of a superstition they had in common with the natives more to the north of the island, namely, that if a man lives in the house of an enemy he has killed in battle, he will be haunted by the dead man's spirit. The houses were beautifully made, and far superior to any I had seen before in New Britain; they were of a semicircular shape, with the roof sloping down to the ground at the back, and the front filled in by beautifully constructed wicker-work, having a small door. The inside of each house was really very well decorated, with figures and designs, some burnt into the wood, others stained in with dyes, made from the juices of various nuts.

The village itself was built in a circle, with an open space in the centre, which was planted with small trees and variegated plants. I cannot account for the village being thus depopulated in any other manner than that the natives who were now showing it to us must have surprised it at night, thus catching all the inhabitants asleep.

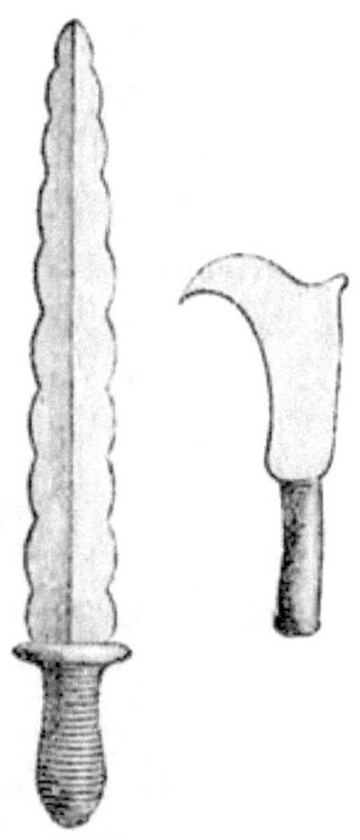

SWORD AND CLUB, SPACIOUS BAY, NEW BRITAIN.

We bought a good many curious implements of war and ornaments from these natives; they had shields, really very cleverly ornamented, and their spears were the most dangerous weapons of that description I have seen in New Britain, the points of them being tipped with a cassowary's claw, only fastened on with a kind of wax or gum; so that when the spear entered the body, the cement would be melted by the heat, and on the weapon being drawn out, the cassowary's claw be left embedded in the flesh. Their clubs are varied in shape, some being well carved, with knobs all round the end, and some, like one Mr. Brown bought, shaped

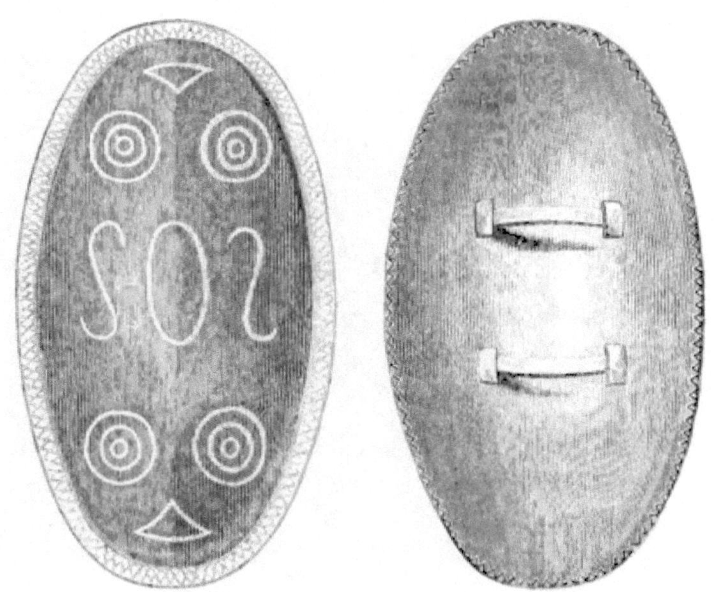

SHIELD, SPACIOUS BAY, NEW BRITAIN.

exactly like a billhook, though where they can have got the idea from I cannot imagine.

Some of the ornaments were fairly well carved: these were tortoise-shell earrings, armlets of the same materials or made of the spiral conch-shell, and curious masks made of network, and cleverly worked in with feathers, which they stretch over their faces when dancing. They also wore a very neatly-stained waist-cloth marked in very good patterns, in most cases with red, yellow, and black. In bartering with the people I found they did not know the use of the iron hoop, so much prized in New Guinea by the natives, nor did they seem to care about a trade tomahawk when I showed it to them, they themselves using stone tomahawks. They would only barter

EARRING, SPACIOUS BAY.

with us for beads and red cloth, a circumstance seeming to me pretty conclusive that they can have had very little intercourse with white men.

Return Point, at the bottom of Spacious Bay, was the furthest spot we visited on this side of the coast. Captain Hunter mentions Spacious Bay in these words: "At noon we found ourselves ten miles to the E.S.E. of Cape Buller before a deep embayment which exists between Cape Buller and Cape Orford, which in this part must reduce the connection north of New Britain to a narrow isthmus. The deep and spacious bay spoken of above was not sufficiently explored to affirm that it does not disconnect the two portions of New Britain ; but if so the channel must be narrow, and was not distinguished from the offing."

After this excursion to Spacious Bay we returned to Makada Harbour (Duke of York Island), where we lay some few days. It was now May. One morning I was awoke by feeling and hearing something grating violently against the ship's side, and running up on deck found the whole of the harbour covered with huge blocks of pumice-stone, and indeed as far as I could see over towards New Britain the sea was covered ; it really appeared as though one could walk to New Britain on it, or, as one of the natives expressed it, " as though the bottom of the sea had jumped up."

We then heard that a great eruption had taken place in the volcano situated at the foot of the Mother Mountain, and the smoke and fire could be plainly seen from Duke of York Island. Next day we set out for Blanche Peninsula, in order to get a nearer view of the sight, but we found we had to go a long way round to the northward, to avoid the enormous fields of pumice-stone that had been drifted down the channel.

It seemed almost impossible that such a large quantity could have been ejected from one volcano, without blowing up the whole surrounding country. We landed to the north of Nodup, and climbed the "Mother," which was to windward of the volcano, and therefore safe from the stones and cinders. From our situation we could gaze down into the fiery crater beneath. In the evening the sight became more than grand—it was awful; every few moments there would come a huge convulsion, and then the very bowels of the earth seemed to be vomited from the crater into the air; enormous stones, red hot, the size of an ordinary house, would be thrown up, almost out of sight, when they would burst like a rocket, and fall hissing into the sea. At the same time angry flames would dart up, almost to the altitude on which we stood, and of the most dazzling brightness. Then all would die down to a low, sulphureous breathing, spreading a blue flame all over the mouth of the crater, whilst over us and all the country near hung a panoply of thick black smoke, broken only by the falling of red-hot stones in showers, which destroyed all vegetation to leeward to a distance of about two miles.

At the first outbreak of this eruption there rose in one night on the W. shore of Blanche Bay an island of about two miles in extent, and seventy feet high, having a crater in the centre filled with boiling water. The new island is semicircular in form, having on its N.E. side a short reef or spur of rocks, terminated by a small island covered with bushes. The new island is at least five miles from the volcano, and those who were on Matupi Island that night state

that a line of fire rose through the water, across
Blanche Bay, from the volcano to where the island
rose.   Large numbers of fish and turtle were picked
up on the surrounding shores quite dead.

This eruption, I am of opinion, caused the tidal
wave that immediately succeeded, and which washed
away a large part of the shore of Matupi Island.
May not other tidal waves arise from a similar cause?
For instance, in the Atlantic, when a submarine
volcano bursts, and the concussion causes an upheaval as in the case of a torpedo, with this difference,
that the depth of the water being so great in the case
of the submarine volcano, it is unable to throw its
force through it into the air, which is therefore
expended on the surrounding volume of water, and
expands in a circle, thus forming a so-called tidal
wave.

About a week after the new island had risen, we
attempted to land, and found the surface still too *hot*
to allow us to stand still upon it ; we had to keep on
moving quickly to prevent our feet being burnt.
The water in the crater was still boiling, and throwing up large quantities of steam.   The eruption of
the volcano lasted upwards of a month, and the
whole of Blanche Bay and a great part of St.
George's Channel were so thickly covered with
pumice-stone, that it was impossible for a vessel, and
a boat only with great difficulty, to force a way
through.   There is no doubt that these fields of
pumice-stone have given rise to the report of many
reefs that have been searched for afterwards with-

out success, for I defy even a practised eye to tell one from the other.

The pumice hangs together in large masses by capillary attraction, bearing with it sometimes branches that have been torn from the trees in its descent; and there settles round the edge of this floating mass a white foam, caused by the incessant washing of the water and the grinding together of the blocks of pumice. This in the distance appears identical with breakers. These fields are carried along by the currents until finally thrown on some shore or broken up by a storm. I have seen an experienced captain keep away from a tide-rip, fearing it was a reef; how much more likely, then, are these fields to be mistaken for them, with so very similar an appearance!

The natives of Matupi and all those living in the vicinity of the volcano left before the eruption began, warned by the shocks of earthquake that preceded it. The Mother and Daughter's Peninsula, on which the volcano is situated, and which gets its name from the mountains so called, bounds Blanche Bay on the N.E. side; it is terminated by Praed Point, so called by H.M.S. *Blanche*.

A little further along the S. end of the peninsula, and immediately under the South Daughter, is a small indentation in the coast, where the *Blanche* anchored, which is called Albino Bay on account of a false report of there being a white woman on the shore there. She turned out to be an Albino woman; these persons are not uncommon in the South Seas, being not unlike a white person, except that the skin appears much pinker, and has an unhealthy look. I have seen some cases where the Albino was piebald, with patches of the light skin intermixed with the natural dark colour. The children of these people seldom retain the parents' peculiarity, but have the ordinary dark skin of their race.

CHAPTER VI.

I TRUST Mr. Brown will forgive me for writing the
following account of an important event, for though
it appeared to the public to be solely his action, yet
in reality Mr. Brown was the last person (connected
with the occurrence) to allow that severe measures
were necessary, and the most unwilling to do so—
severe measures which were absolutely necessary to
save the lives of nearly all the foreigners in these
parts, those, namely, of some twenty Fijian and
Samoan missionary teachers, their wives and children
who were specially under Mr. Brown's charge, inas-
much as he had brought them from their own
countries to show to the New Britain people the
light of the Gospel ; there were also Mr. Brown's
own wife and children, besides several white traders
on various parts of the coast of New Britain, who

would have been certainly included in the general massacre, on account of their trade being an object of ambition to the natives.

On the 8th of April, 1878, our little vessel was lying in Port Hunter (N. of Duke of York Island) under repairs, having been stripped of her rigging, when a messenger came on board from Mr. Brown saying he would be glad to see me at his house, and accordingly I immediatly went up there. We had heard a rumour two or three days before amongst the natives that four of the teachers had been murdered, but I had not attached much importance to it, as these sorts of reports were common enough. But Mr. Brown had told me that when he first heard it he felt it *must* be true, by the terrible misgivings he felt at heart. However, on this morning Ratu Levi and two other teachers had arrived at his house with the sad news, and Mr. Brown had kindly asked me to be present whilst they gave their account.

I found on my arrival Mr. Brown sitting in a chair, Ratu Levi and the other two teachers seated on the ground in front of him, and their faces wore a look of sorrowful determination.   Mr. Brown rose to meet me, and as he shook hands he said, " I knew it was true, they are murdered and eaten."   Then Ratu Levi told the sad story, Mr. Brown kindly translating, as he spoke in Fijian.   The story was in the main as follows :—

Two parties of teachers had received permission from Mr. Brown to make an excursion into the interior; they had some of them, I understood, previously visited these villages inland, which they now wished to revisit, and had been very well received, being also invited to return there again; and it was this invitation they were complying with on this last occasion. Mr. Brown had given them a few beads, to make presents to the chiefs of the villages visited, and they had arranged to start in two parties, one from Blanche Bay, the other from Tarlily Bay (Ruterwool), meet inland and return together. The party that started from Reuterwool consisted of Sailasa, a Fijian native minister; Livai Naboro, Fijian teacher; Timote and Beni, both teachers. The other party, starting from Blanche Bay, were Ratu Levi and two more teachers. After the latter had travelled a little way inland, a native woman warned them they had better not go on, as if they did the natives would kill them, and afterwards added, "as they have another party." Ratu Levi and his companions therefore retraced their steps, and this time made their guide walk in front of them, warning him that if they saw any signs of treachery they should kill him. Thus they arrived safely at Blanche Bay again, though had they persisted in going on they would undoubtedly have shared the fate of their companions. Then these fine fellows started off from Blanche Bay across the narrow neck of land to Goonan to make inquiries at Ruterwool. It was there they learnt that the report was indeed but too true, and that the wives and children of the murdered men were in imminent danger, as the chief, Tarlily, stated that he intended making prisoners of them all. Had this occurred how terrible would have been their fate! Sailasa's daughter, we understood, was to be Tarlily's concubine, and the little children and elder women would have perished under the club of the cannibal to serve as a repast for the triumphant savage.

The narrators also told how the four teachers had met with their death, which they had learnt from natives who witnessed it. Tarlily, knowing the teachers were going inland, and fearing by their means trade might be carried to inland villages, who had hitherto only been able to obtain it through him —knowing also, coward that he was, that the teachers were unarmed—thought to make large profit by selling joints of their dead bodies to surrounding villages for "taboo" (native money). He allowed them to get well inland, paying, however, both some of his men to follow them and chiefs of certain inland villages to assist in the murder. Thus these poor unsuspecting men passed through Tarlily's village, being received by him in an apparently very friendly manner.

As the teachers got further inland many natives followed them, to whom Sailasa preached, and towards evening, finding themselves on a small rising hill, they knelt down there to say their evening prayers. This was the moment chosen by the cowardly murderers for their attack, and Timote was the first to fall with a spear through him from back to breast. When Sailasa saw this, he appeared to be so overcome with sorrow, for Timote was not much more than a lad, and had been entrusted to Sailasa's special charge by his friends in Fiji, that when Beni called upon him to defend himself, he answered, "Timote is dead, it is better that I follow him." However, he was not the next to fall, as Livai Naboro received his death-blow immediately after Timote; Sailasa being the last to fall at that spot, pierced with many spears.

Beni, who was a very powerful young man, and was also armed with a fowling-piece (though I believe he never had an opportunity of loading it), fought his way like a lion down as far as Tarlily's village, where he thought himself safe and with a friendly chief, for Tarlily came out to ask what was the matter. Beni then asked for some water to drink, which was brought him, and as his head was thrown back in the act of drinking, Tarlily, with one sweep of his large knife, nearly severed the head from the body.

The bodies of these four poor men were then sold in pieces to the inhabitants of all villages anxious to buy them, and Tarlily's next move was to determine to obtain the wives and children of the slain, who were together at Ruterwool in Sailasa's house awaiting the return of their friends. Immediately on learning the truth Ratu Levi and his companions had come over to Mr. Brown and now asked him (after narrating this terrible story that I have given you) what he intended to do. Mr. Brown replied, "I shall start at once for Ruterwool, and bring away the women and children ; I cannot move the men, they must stay." This Ratu Levi quite agreed to, as had Mr. Brown removed the teachers from Ruterwool it would have been certain to provoke an attack on all the rest in other parts of the island. "Nothing succeeds like success" is very true with regard to these natives; and Tarlily, flushed with the success of his first enterprise, would immediately, on the smallest sign of fear amongst the foreigners, certainly have attacked them all. Or had Mr. Brown removed a teacher, it would have been interpreted into a sign of fear on his part, and a general attack might have been expected on all sides, and the different stations, both missionary and trading, being so far apart, would have been unable to help each other, and would therefore have fallen a prey to the natives one by one.

Thus it behoved Mr. Brown to show no signs of fear, and, moreover, he had but one leaky boat, which could not have carried even a quarter of the number of teachers, even supposing the boat could have accomplished the two hundred miles requisite. Also, had the teachers gone, it would have been leaving the white traders alone, and could have had but one ultimate result, viz., the death of all. Mr. Brown's steam launch was quite unavailable, having, I believe, a hole in her boiler or something equally disabling. My little vessel was stripped of her rigging, and could not have been ready under a fortnight. However, Mr. Brown started at once for Ruterwool, taking with him the three teachers that had brought

the news, and a few trustworthy Duke of York
natives as crew. He reached Ruterwood that
same evening only just in time. Tarlily's men
were actually at the fence surrounding the teacher's
house, where the women and children had been left
in charge of one teacher and one Duke of York
boy, and these two brave fellows were preparing to
make a desperate resistance.

The natives all decamped on the arrival of Mr.
Brown, who immediately began making arrangements for the removal of the women and children.
He sent a messenger to Tarlily, telling them he was
there, and if Tarlily could come down and speak to
him, he (Mr. Brown) would guarantee his safety.
The messenger presently returned with Tarlily's
answers, which were to the effect that he (Tarlily)
had eaten four of Mr. Brown's teachers, and, further,
intended to eat them all, as well as Mr. Brown and
all white men on the island. He, moreover, informed Mr. Brown that the taro was cooking with
which to eat *him*. This was the main part of the
message, but it was also mixed with horrible refer-
ences to the wives of Mr. Brown and the teachers,
and other hideous ideas which only a cannibal can
express.

There was but one alternative, namely, that the
wives and children of the murdered men should be
delivered up to him—on this condition only would
Tarlily make peace. He further stated that men-of-
war might come, he did not care for *them*, they only
came for pigs and yams, as there was not enough

food in their own country (!); he did not care for muskets, he could dodge the bullets; men-of-war would be afraid to follow him into the bush. This is his speech as it was told me, and though it *may* have been somewhat added to, owing to the excitement, still I do not think it was so, as I have had just such a message myself *verbatim.*

Mr. Brown then sent, I believe, to other chiefs about, trying to induce them to reason with Tarlily, but all to no purpose, so he then left, taking with him the wives and children of the murdered men, Ratu Levi and the other teachers following in canoes as far as Nodup. In the meanwhile the teachers on Duke of York Island had held a large council at Mowlot, and appointed Ratu Levi (who was in reality a chief, " Ratu " signifying " chief " in Fijian) their spokesman. He informed Mr. Brown that the teachers had agreed to defend themselves by assuming the aggressive, and not to wait for Tarlily to murder them one by one. They trusted that Mr. Brown would assist them, but even if he would not do so *they* were determined to attack Tarlily themselves. They were also determined to obtain the bones of their murdered friends, in order to give them Christian burial. Meanwhile in Mr. Brown's absence the Duke of York natives became excessively insolent to Mrs. Brown, and came demanding beads, red cloth, &c., from her. News also came from New Ireland that a chief, hearing of the murder of teachers in New Britain, had seized the wife of one of the teachers stationed there, and that

her husband had only just escaped himself by having
a musket and showing fight with it. Thus things
were beginning to look as bad as could be on all
sides; everywhere the natives seemed to have a
general feeling that they could now look down on
whites and treat them with insolence. So immediately on Mr. Brown's return to Duke of York a
council was held, at which it was determined that if
we wished to save our lives we must either fight,
and fight well, or withdraw altogether from these
islands at once. As this latter plan was impossible,
the former was the only alternative, and Mr. Brown
at last was obliged unwillingly to admit that it must
be so. I at once lent all my available muskets and
ammunition to arm the teachers, as did some of the
traders, and on the 16th we started for Nodup (New
Britain), where we were to pick up a number of
Torrortooroo's men to act as scouts and guides.
These men were of immense use to us, as they not
only acted as scouts and guides, but foraged for us,
and did picket work as well; we armed them with
some of my smooth-bore " Brown Besses." From
Nodup we proceeded to Matupi, which was to be the
head-quarters of the landing party. There we held
a further council, when it was decided that the
teachers with the Nodup contingent were to land on
the Blanche Bay side of Goonan and march down
into Tarlily's country and also to surrounding
villages, the natives of which had either assisted in
the murder or eaten any portions of the bodies.
They were to burn their villages, destroy their

plantations, and disperse bodies of natives sent against us by Tarlily or his allies, but to be very careful that no women or children were injured either in fighting or in burning the huts. It was also clearly given out that any natives accompanying the expedition and *attempting* cannibalism would be considered as enemies and treated accordingly. Further, that all friendly natives joining or following the expedition must wear a piece of white calico on the right arm, any native omitting to do so to be treated as an enemy. White strips of calico having been distributed to the natives of Nodup and Matupi, Mr. Brown was to go round to Ruterwool and Tarlily Bay, to prevent any escape of natives by water on that side to Man Island. Mr. Brown had already obtained assurance from Bu-lilli, the powerful chief of Kabakadaie, that he would assist him and send his fighting men to attack Tarlily from that side (Kabakadaie lies between Junior Mission House Point and Shoal Point, extending for some distance inland). The orders were duly given to the friendly chiefs, and by them communicated to those of their men who were to join the expedition, as well as to all who might be likely to follow. This being done, Mr. Brown determined to make one last effort at con-ciliation by sending another message to Tarlily and to the chiefs of each village implicated, requesting them to pay for the murdered teachers, and return their bones. This request for payment may sound strange to civilised ears, and seem a somewhat savage way of compensating for murder, but in reality it is not so to those who understand these natives. They would really sooner lose fifty men by fighting than one hundred fathoms of " taboo," and there is no surer way of punishing them than by taking their money. This was therefore Mr. Brown's intention when he demanded restitution in shell money for his murdered teachers. Outsiders might call our determination to fight revenge, but in reality it was not so, it was simply to save our lives ; but at the same time it was an action to be avoided by *missionaries* were any other means possible. Had Tarlily therefore paid the money it would have been equivalent to acknowledging himself beaten or in the wrong, and so the prestige of the missionaries and the white men would have been restored without bloodshed.

There were two sides to the question of our action, and I think most people have been inclined to judge it by only one, though certainly it was that side most apparent to those far distant from the scene. One side, and the side *we* wished to show the natives at that time, was that we were capable of fighting as well as they were, and that as they had *made* us fight they must take the consequences. Another motive for us was that we were fighting for the lives of women and children, our own lives and our property ; but this latter was not the reason to give our enemies, lest they should take advantage of it in the future when foreigners might not be so numerous in the island as they were then. The world did not see this side of the question, but judged simply by what it saw, and *that* looked very like revenge.

As I said before with regard to these natives, " Nothing succeeds like success," therefore Tarlily refused our proposals, and answered much in his former boastful manner. We waited quietly at Matupi till the 17th for all the answers to come in ; they were all much in the same strain as Tarlily's, therefore it was finally decided that the attack should be made early next morning before daylight, so as to get well into the enemies' country before they were aware that we had commenced operations. As soon as this was settled, Mr. Brown started away in his boat, accompanied by a trader, Mr. Blohm, in order to be at their position (on the coast of Ruterwool) by daybreak.

At two o'clock A.M. on the 18th we were all ready and started in canoes and a trader's boat over to the New Britain coast at the head of Blanche Bay, landing at a spot immediately opposite Goonan. This was in a district not actually implicated in the murders, and was the best place for massing our forces, as the people were to a certain extent friendly, yet no doubt had they seen us at any time getting the worst of it they would at once have joined the enemy. It was a strange sight to see canoe after canoe landing its freight of dusky savages in perfect silence, one small fire shedding a fitful light upon us all. Under a tree near the beach we held our last council, standing all armed. Our small force consisted of Ratu Levi, with twenty teachers, eighteen fully armed Nodup natives, several Matupi natives, two other white men and myself, making a total of about sixty actual fighting men. Of course there were a great many followers, who came merely to see the fighting and obtain loot, but these were not to be counted on as helpers, for probably at the first attack they would all run off. The guides were then told that if they showed any signs of treachery they would be shot; if on the other hand they were faithful, a large present would be made them.

We then started on our march up the high range of hills that runs like a backbone from the "North Daughter" southwards to Ruterwool, the ascent being made in the same district from which we had started, and the guides leading the way with long sticks in their hands to probe the tracks for pits. These pits are dug by the natives a little on one side of the track, and they place spears at the bottom and sides, covering them with long grass and leaves; the reason for their digging them on one side being that the enemy stepping on the edge will be precipitated sideways into the pit, which ensures his falling on the spears, whereas were the pit in the middle of the path he might fall forward and save himself by clinging to the side.

Another method is to conceal two spears in the high grass, one on each side of the track, with the points towards the direction from which an attack is expected; to the head of each spear is fastened an end of a very fine but very strong piece of line.

This line catches an advancing enemy just above the waist, and his forward movement draws both the spears forcibly into the body. The latter plan is a very dangerous one, especially to any one moving quickly. The natives also place spear-points and pieces of split bamboo in the road; these run through the foot like a knife if one happens to tread on them, and a boot will hardly save you. I do not think there was a boot to be found in all our little army; so the guides were of the utmost importance when fighting with these natives. They are generally very experienced warriors, and have to be paid better than other fighting men, as they commonly bear the brunt of an attack.

About daybreak we entered the enemies' country, marching in Indian file, which is necessitated by the narrowness of the tracks, and also on account of following the guides. On reaching the fighting ground we threw out scouts or skirmishers on each flank, to guard against surprise on either hand; these were the Nodup natives. The first village we came to we immediately set fire to; by this time it was pretty light, and the smoke was a signal that the fighting had commenced both to friends and foes. This village was deserted saving one or two spies dodging about amongst the bananas. There was nothing to be seen of the main body of natives. They had evidently received warning of our approach. We fired upon the spies, and cut down the bananas. Then we went on, burning each village as we came to it, the natives making very little stand, merely slinging stones and throwing spears from a distance.

At ten A.M. we were in Kabakadaie, and before noon at the head of Port Webber, having marched twenty-five miles and burnt at least twenty villages in less than ten hours. We then doubled, and came back by a different route into the very centre of Tarlily's land, and at noon we halted at a single house that stood on a hill, surrounded with cocoa-nut trees, having on one side a patch of thick scrub, and here we determined to have dinner. Had we thought first, we should have seen what a disadvantageous spot it was in the case of an attack, as the ground that was covered with scrub was slightly above the open spot on which we were camped.

We were just in the middle of eating our food, consisting of yams, taro, and fowls, taken from the different villages we had burnt, and our arms were laid aside, when one of the scouts came running in to say that a body of men of about two hundred under Tarlily were coming up the other side of the hill under cover of the scrub. He had hardly finished speaking when we were assaulted by a shower of stones from their slings, one of which passed a few inches above my head and buried itself in the stump of a cocoa-nut tree, showing with what terrific force they fly.

The stones were accompanied by a few rifle shots, so that now was the time to see who were really to be depended upon. Most of the natives who had been following us all day when things had been all smooth ran off down the hill as fast as they could. However, it did not take long to get our arms ready, and charge out on the enemy. It was a sharp skirmish while it lasted, which was not for long, as we soon dislodged them from the batch of scrub and drove them down the hill. However, they really fought well and showed some good manœuvring. As soon as they were on clear ground, they opened out into a sort of skirmishing order, though not of course with much regularity, and retreated down hill in this manner, keeping up a storm of stones with their slings and occasionally firing a rifle. We pressed them hard, keeping a sort of open order also, to avoid giving them much mark to aim at.

There were a large number of them fully armed with slings, spears, and tomahawks; some few had muskets also. It is a most reprehensible practice, that of selling muskets to savages, as it makes them much more dangerous than they naturally are, and that is bad enough. We followed them at the double, only halting to fire, which must have been pretty precise, to judge from the bodies we passed. At the bottom of the hill they gave way altogether, turning and running for the thick bush. We made one final charge as we too reached the bottom of the hill, and the Nodup natives set up a war-cry of triumph.

I had then time to look round and see who were with us, and found that there were only the Nodup and a few of the Matupi natives. I don't think our force was more than sixty altogether, and though up to this time there had been quite three hundred natives following as professed friends, they only came to loot, and decamped on the slightest alarm. We did not follow the enemy into the bush, but returned to finish our dinner, leaving the Nodup natives to watch Tarlily's movements. He, I am sorry to say, was not killed, but was wounded in the arm—I hope sufficiently to assure him that he could *not* dodge " the white men's bullets " as easily as he supposed.

After dinner we determined that we had done enough for one day, we therefore moved on about a mile to a hill crowned with cocoa-nut trees but with clear ground all round, which was a more suitable place to form a camp for the night. By degrees the natives, who had left us on the first alarm, came back, and set to work preparing for the night. Then came one of the most curious sights I have ever seen—the natives went out in parties, and brought back *houses* with them, the posts of which, being only driven a short way into the ground, were easily lifted out, and the house was then carried to our encampment! so that in a short space of time this spot, that had been destitute of anything in the shape of a dwelling, was covered with native huts, and each hut had at least one fire burning by it, and this in the darkness of the night presented a most weird appearance. I could quite have fancied that a town had sprung up by magic; indeed, when I saw the first house coming along apparently by itself, I was utterly taken aback for a moment. The grass was set fire shortly after we arrived, in order to burn a clear space round us.

The Nodup natives were out on all sides, watching for spies, and every now and then we heard a musket shot away in the distance, which showed that they were on the alert. Indeed, the way these men performed this duty was splendid, it could not have been better done. They crept through the long grass from place to place, not a movement seemed to escape them, and every now and then they would come in and report. It appeared that Tarlily's party were watching us very closely in order to take advantage of any opportunity that might occur for attacking us.

I had made arrangements with Mr. Brown to fire a rocket as soon as it was dark in order to show him that we were all right. However, although we fired it, it would not go up, but went hissing down amongst the grass. This was very disappointing, as there were no other means of communicating to him that all was well; indeed, I think it *was* a wonderful thing that not one of our party had been hurt.

Next morning we were up betimes, about four o'clock, and again on the march to Karavia, a large town situated above the N.E. coast of Blanche Bay, which rises from the bay to a height of eight hundred feet, and it is on the top of these hills that Upper Karavia is situated. Lower Karavia is about three miles lower down near the coast.

The country as we approached Upper Karavia was beautiful open table-land, spreading as far as we could see on either side, only broken here and there by groups of cocoa-nut palms and small clumps of other trees, denoting in most cases small villages or single huts. We had a long march of about ten miles, during which we burnt several small villages and had one sharp skirmish with the natives, who appeared to be congregating at Karavia to give us a warm reception. This party with which we had the skirmish was undoubtedly a scouting party sent to find out where we were and to check our advance, in order to give the natives time to hide their taboo. But in this latter attempt they did not succeed, for we continued to advance in spite of their sling stones, and as they had no intention of coming to a hand-to-hand encounter, they kept retreating in front of us. In order, therefore, to get rid of them we charged at them, when they turned and fled.

Great caution was required in approaching Karavia, as this could only be effected from inland by two entrances on account of the thick bush by which it was surrounded. We therefore divided into two parties, in order to attack the town by each entrance. It was evident that they were ready for us, although I think they had hardly expected us so soon, as there was great shouting and beating of tom-toms. Whether Tarlily was there in person I never discovered, but I almost fancy he must have been.

One of our two parties consisted of Ratu Levi and most of the teachers, with the Matupi men; the other of the Nodup natives, the remainder of the teachers.

myself, and one other white man. We found the
entrance we had to pass in at was blocked by having
a quantity of prickly palms pulled down over the
path. This with bare feet was anything but pleasant,
but the enemy was in front, and we were not to be
stopped by thorns, yet great care had to be observed
for fear of spear points or pieces of bamboo. As we
got towards the town we could hear that there were
a great number of natives there, and determined to
give them a volley as soon as we were inside the
belt of bush and could see them, also before they
had time to attack us with their spears and stones.
So we dashed in upon them and fired; the place
seemed to be full of howling demons, who threw
spears by the dozen, though without much aim, as
none of our party were hit.

After firing our first volley, we reloaded as quickly
as possible under cover of the trees, and then
began a kind of independent firing, so that those
who had loaded could cover those that were loading.
We could see that several natives dropped, though
the remainder stood fast, encouraged by the women,
who looked like devils, jumping about and dancing
and shouting out defiance and abuse of the most
disgusting kind.

In the meantime spears and stones were being
showered amongst us, and I felt we could not last
any time at this, as some of our party must be hit
before long. I could not think what had become of
our other party, for we had as yet seen no signs of
them, and I was beginning to feel very anxious; but

the Nodup natives behaved splendidly, with old Torrortooroo encouraging them, telling them to fire true, and calling them his boys, going from one to the other, only stopping now and then to fire when he saw a good opportunity. When he fired I always noticed an enemy dropped.

We must have kept on at this nearly half-an-hour when suddenly we heard a heavy volley of musketry some distance to the right of us. I never was better pleased in my life than to hear that sound, as we could not have held our position much longer without losing some of our men. As it was I cannot understand how some one was not hit, the stones and spears were falling so thickly all round us.

As soon as the enemy heard the firing of a second party, they seemed to become quite demoralised; they undoubtedly thought that in fighting the first party they were fighting all. We saw that they were giving way, and pushed them harder, advancing as they retired, and soon they were running helter-skelter down the hill-side below their town. The fight lasted altogether about an hour, after which there was not an enemy to be seen, save those that would never eat human flesh again : these were all buried in holes we dug in the ground. Great quantities of taboo were found in and around the town, which was taken as spoil. Here we had something to eat, and then proceeded down the hills towards the coast, to attack Lower Karavia.

On the way we found a poor little baby, which the mother had thrown away, and doubtless had the native looting party accompanying us found it they would have killed the poor little thing. We, however, had it carried with us, giving it to a boy, telling him that if he did not bring it down to the coast in safety, he would have to answer for it with his life, but if he brought it down in safety he would be paid for it. It appears that the mother was escaping with the child and a bundle of taboo, and that, rather than lose the shell-money, she threw her baby away, as one of the teachers, not knowing it was a woman, was chasing her.

I may here state, that with my own eyes I did not see the dead body of one woman, and I do not know that one was killed, which speaks well for our native contingent, as the women are hard to distinguish from the men at any distance, and they also take quite as prominent a part in the fighting as the men. It was in this village that some of Sailasa's bones were found, but how they were determined to be his bones I cannot explain; however, the teachers said that they were, and of course that was sufficient.

The whole town was soon in a blaze, and we again marching to Lower Karavia. This was a somewhat dangerous route, as we had to pass through a deep ravine, with overhanging sides, which, had the natives been more used to this mode of warfare, they would have taken advantage of, by rolling down big stones on us from above. As it was, however, we passed through without any opposition, though we saw a large body of natives watching us from some distance away. These quickly dispersed on having a few muskets discharged at them. We were now approaching Lower Karavia, having burnt many villages on the way, and as we entered the town we could see the natives escaping in their canoes, leaving the town in our undisputed possession, which we were heartily glad of, as we had had enough of fighting.

After burning Lower Karavia we camped on the shore, to await the boat and canoes from Matupi to take us back there, as it was determined to leave the other places for a future date, and also give them a chance to surrender and pay their fine. We had given Tarlily such a lesson as he was not likely to forget, and which we hoped might be a warning to the villages of Dewawon and Dinawon, the two principal places still unburnt that were implicated in the murder and eating of the teachers.

On arriving at Matupi I sent a letter to Mr. Brown, telling him of all we had done, and what must have lightened his heart very much, that all were unhurt. He then joined us and explained that the reason that we had seen nothing of Bu-lilli (the chief who had promised to attack Tarlily from the Ruterwool side) was, that he had not shown up at all. Indeed, as it afterwards appeared, he had received taboo from Tarlily not to fight against him. No doubt, Bu-lilli thought that we should not be able to stand against Tarlily by ourselves; however, it was shown by the sequel that he was much mistaken.

As the 21st was Easter day, we stayed quietly at
Matupi, where Mr. Brown held service and offered a
prayer of thanksgiving for the merciful manner in
which we had been preserved from all harm; in the
evening messages were sent to Dewawon and
Dinawon of a pacific nature, requesting them to pay
the fine and return the bones of the teachers in their
possession, the alternative being that their towns
would share the same fate as the other places, the
natives of which had eaten portions of the teachers
and assisted in the murder. Answers were sent
back daring us to come, and refusing to pay. On
Monday morning, therefore, we started for Dewawon,
which lies on rising ground a little on the west side
of the south bight of Blanche Bay.

In the meantime two traders from Ruterwool and
Kabakadaie had joined us at Matupi with their boats,
which were very acceptable for taking some of the
party over to the mainland instead of having to use
canoes; moreover, we now had Mr. Brown's boat, and
one from Makada, in all four boats, and these, with a
number of canoes, formed our fleet of transports.
We had also a really stronger fighting party than
before, having been reinforced by Mr. Brown's party
as well as by the two traders who had not deemed it
prudent to leave their stations whilst the fighting
was going on in *their* direction, but who now that so
decisive a blow had been given to Tarlily felt sure
he would attempt no more attacks upon the foreigners
for the present. They had therefore come over to
help us as soon as safety permitted.

We landed just below Dewawon, and climbed the steep hill leading up to it in two parties, intending to attack the town on each side. However, there was no resistance made whatever, as the natives appeared to have left everything and run away into the bush. I cannot understand what reason they had for sending so defiant a message as they did if they had no intention of braving it out. There was much taboo found and many curiosities in the huts, which were taken as spoils of war, and the town was soon in a blaze.

We then moved on rapidly upon Dinawon; this place is about three to four miles further on inland, yet reaches down to the water's edge in the extreme head of the south bight of Blanche Bay. The main part of the town is inland and surrounded by thick bush and cocoa-nut trees. In the only open space a few of us halted on a small hillock, from which place we could see the whole of our forces winding up the hill, and it was a very strange sight. First came the armed party, then a number of natives with spears and tomahawks, and after them an apparently innumerable number of natives carrying all manner of spoil taken from Dewawon—pigs, poultry, yams, taro, ornaments, spears, and clubs decorated with parrots' feathers; others with dogs caught about the huts, which are considered a great delicacy by these natives; again, two men would be carrying huge bunches of bananas or cocoa-nuts slung upon a bamboo and carried on their shoulders; some, again, would have tame cockatoos or parrots in their hands;

others had large basketsful of taboo—in fact, every conceivable thing that is to be found in and around a native town.

I here found a very curious article, which previous to this I was not aware had any existence in these islands, viz., a dead man's paddle, which is buried with him to enable him to paddle his way across the water to the sky or horizon, which is where they imagine the sky touches the water. From whence they get the canoe does not appear, but I suppose the spirit steals it from the shore tribes; this superstition is not found amongst them, however, but only with the bushmen or natives of the interior. These paddles are large and flat, very elaborately carved, and ornamented with that curious face-like ornament that is the same looked at either way, up or down, and which occurs so often amongst the decorations of these people. The handle is long and also carved in an irregular triangulated pattern with lines running diagonally. The whole is rubbed over with white lime, which fills the crevices of the pattern and makes it show white against the dark wood. Considering the tools these people work with, I think it is very wonderful they turn out such good work; these tools I will describe further on. I found on inquiry that the Karavia people joined with our party, and were actually guiding those they were at war with two days before to make war on a tribe that had been their friends—thus showing that nature is stronger than colour, and that "join with the stronger to oppose the weaker" is as true a maxim with these savages as it is with the civilised white man.

At Dinawon we had very little trouble to possess ourselves of the town; a few rounds of musketry, and all the natives ran away, leaving the whole place in our possession. Here also we found a good deal of spoil in the way of curiosities, clubs, spears, nets for fishing, &c. These were confiscated, and the place burnt, as well as any huts that were passed on the way down to the beach; each hut on every occasion was carefully examined to see that there was no one in it, besides being entered by natives in search for loot. I am glad to say we saved one old native woman from being killed by a native of Karavia, who had found her in a hut, left evidently by the owners, who were in too great haste to get away (when they saw us coming) to remove her.

We heard a loud screaming, and on coming up found a native of Karavia just about to split her skull open with his tomahawk.

I told him I had a good mind to knock his brains out, and that if he did not take himself off immediately I should do so. We then placed two men on guard over the hut, to prevent its being burnt, as the old woman could not get away, being too infirm. The men remained by it until all the other houses were burnt, leaving the woman to her friends when they returned; hers being the only house that was left standing of any place we had visited during the whole expedition.

I have often wondered whether the natives appreciated that little act of humanity, but I fear they could hardly understand it.   On arriving at the beach we found Mr. Brown waiting in his boat, all the three other boats and the canoes waiting to take us off; indeed, I was very glad it was all over, as my feet were in such a state with thorns, cuts, and bruises, that I could not have done another day's march had I tried.

We returned at once to Matupi to stay the night. About seven o'clock that evening a number of chiefs came over to see Mr. Brown, to declare their sub-mission, and bringing some of the bones of the murdered men.

They also brought taboo, in order to pay the fine.

Mr. Brown told them that had they paid it in the first instance they could have saved bloodshed and their houses and plantations.

They said, " We did not know; it was not fighting—it was an earthquake."

Mr. Brown would not take more than one roll of taboo, and that was to show that friendship was again established between us and them.   They also begged Mr. Brown to send them a teacher to each village of which they were chiefs; indeed, during the next few weeks requests of this kind were constantly coming to Mr. Brown, in some instances from tribes we had never heard of before.   However, Mr. Brown had not sufficient teachers to send to half of them.

The only chief that did not submit was Tarlily, the greatest offender, though Mr. Brown sent to him, promising him perfect safety if he would come and see him.   He was afterwards several times on board my vessel, but I never could persuade him to accompany me to Duke of York Island in order to hold an interview with Mr. Brown.

Indeed, later on he burnt one of the missionary teacher's houses that had been built at Kabakadaie, so inveterate was his hatred of missionaries.

I am glad to say, however, this did not extend any further amongst his family, as his son was very friendly with the whites, and was some time on board Hernsheim and Co.'s schooner as a passenger.

I think that many of the troubles that missionaries have to contend with arise from having native teachers. They are but lately reclaimed from savage life themselves, and much of its odour still clings to them ; and they can hardly be expected to have that enormous fund of patience and tact that is required by a missionary.

Moreover, their colour is against them ; their habits also are too much like those they come to live amongst to raise them to that height of superiority that is necessary, for never was maxim made that could apply better than to these people, " Familiarity breeds contempt."

How can the head of a missionary station feel sure that a native teacher will not make use of some expression in a sermon that may offend ; or if he does not offend, make use of some statements that are unadvisable and derogatory to the religion they are striving to teach ?

I myself heard one sermon that I think was any-thing but wise delivered before a chief of some note and a good muster of his tribe, by one of the Fijian teachers.

He was trying to explain how good a thing "lotu," or religion, was.   He said :—

"See what the lotu has done for us—we have houses, we have a big ship to come and visit us, and bring us cloth, beads, &c. Mr. Brown has a big house and is a powerful chief; all this has lotu given us; then how good a thing lotu is—it is better than taboo."

I spoke to the chief afterwards, and he said, " If lotu will give all these things, then it can give taboo also; if they can show me how it will give me taboo I will go to lotu often." Thus a wrong impression was made by a well-intentioned man.

Do not think for one moment that I do not give all credit due to those noble fellows, who try to do their duty as far as their light goes, but what I contend is, that their light is *not sufficient*. White men are undoubtedly the men to send as missionaries to these people ; and if they cannot cover so large a field of work as if native teachers were employed, yet the work they do would be more thoroughly done.

There is one certain advantage in having white men, that if a white teacher was murdered and eaten, his bones would not be likely to be recovered by his fellow white men. There would have to be half-a-dozen Commissioners and a High Commissioner to try the case, and by the time they got to the spot there would be no case to try, because there would be no complainants left !

This would save an immense amount of trouble and expense to the Government, and would make room for other missionaries to share the same fate. Mr. Brown was tried for manslaughter because he could not wait for the High Commissioner.

They received the news in Fiji just *three months* after the occurrence, and it would, no doubt, have taken another two months before the High Commissioner could arrive on the spot ; and by that time where would the foreigners in New Britain have been ?

I think it shows great common sense on the part of the authorities that they acquitted Mr. Brown.

The effect upon the natives on all sides was marvellous ; they were civil, tractable, and obliging ; no danger was now apprehended from travelling where before it would have been the height of folly to go.

I cannot refrain from giving a few of the opinions of the Australian Press, as they really give a very fair and impartial account. I quote from the *Weekly Advocate* of October the 12th, 1878 :—

" We propose, in fulfilment of a promise made a fortnight ago, to notice some of the comments made by the Press, secular and religious, on the recent painful intelligence from the Rev. George Brown. We begin with the leading journal of this colony. It must be borne in mind that the article now in question appeared before the full text of Mr. Brown's lengthy letter was published. In respect to the massacre the *Sydney Morning Herald* says that so much of the civilization of Polynesia has been due to the pioneer work of missionaries, and so much now is still to be hoped for from the same source, that it is much to be deplored that efficient men capable of good service should have fallen victims to the unreduced barbarism of the natives.

" After a sentence in which is expressed a generous appreciation of what Wesleyan missionaries had accomplished in other groups of islands, the *Herald* observes :—

" ' It has always been the case, that the mountain tribes are fiercer than those on the coast, more backward in civilization, more difficult to subdue. Even in Fiji, which has so many years been the scene of missionary operations, the hill tribes have only been brought under control since British authority has been established, and since the Government has had at its disposal an armed force representative of its authority. By missionaries, therefore, hill tribes must always be approached with great caution, or with a fully recognised risk, and prudence matured by experience should always regulate the efforts which energy and devotion inspire. From the brief account which has reached us it is doubtful whether the attempt made to penetrate the interior of the island was not premature.

" ' Enough had scarcely been done to naturalize

civilization and Christianity on the coast to make a further advance politic.

"'The elevated interior will, in days to come, be by preference the residence of European missionaries and settlers, because the climate is likely to be healthier; and, therefore, the conquest of this district to civilization is a matter of importance. But the moral subjugation of the mountain tribes will take much time and much patience.'

"The reply to these remarks is (1) that the interior which was visited by the murdered teachers was not an area of broken hill country, but a level plateau, only dotted with timber, so that 'mountain tribes' in the ordinary acceptation of the words do not exist in that part of the island; and (2) that the massacre was instigated by a coast chief, who possibly would have carried out his diabolical purposes at some other time if no inland expedition had given him the opportunity he actually availed himself of.

"The *Herald* further says: 'But much as the massacre of the missionaries is to be deplored, the retaliation organized and inflicted by the Rev. Mr. Brown is still more to be deplored. That gentleman's statement and explanation are not yet to hand, and his past services and his devotion to the missionary cause claim for him every fair consideration at the hands of hostile critics.

"'But we fear that in treating aggression as the best mode of self-defence he has, as a missionary, committed a serious blunder. This policy may be proper enough in a civil government, though even then it should be carried out with discretion and forbearance towards absolutely uncivilized natives. But Christian missionaries undermine their own special force when they bear the sword. Every missionary who treads untrodden paths goes with his life in his hands, fully conscious of the risk he is running, and prepared, if need be, to be one of those martyrs whose blood is the seed of the Church. Ordinary civilians are not expected or called upon to abstain from self-defence, and we have no right to complain if in protecting their own lives they find it unfortunately necessary to take the life of a barbarian who, from a misunderstanding of the nature of their visit, threatens theirs.

" ' The views thus voiced are doubtless widely held both within and without the Wesleyan denomination, but the editor of this journal—speaking here only for himself—is absolutely unable to understand how it would be right for an ordinary civilian to take the life of a barbarian in self-defence, and yet wrong for a missionary to act after the same fashion.'

" And it should not for a moment be forgotten in this discussion that Mr. Brown was chiefly concerned to protect the lives of his remaining teachers and their families, above all, the widows and orphans of those who fell on the plateau. It is one thing to sacrifice oneself; but what right has any man, missionary or other, to hand over by non-defence a number of helpless women and children to the clubs and ovens of a swarm of cannibal savages?

"We have heard that Tarlily, having eaten Sailasa, the native minister, designed to reserve Sailasa's eldest daughter for a worse fate than the one which overtook her father. Ought Mr. Brown to have contented himself with being a passive spectator of heathen lust and bloodshed?

"The criticism of the *Town and Country Journal,* like that of the last paper quoted, is generous in its tone towards mission work in general and Mr. Brown's labours in particular. We give it entire :— 'The despatches of the Rev. Geo. Brown respecting the recent massacre and retaliation war are marked by a straightforwardness that is commendable. He has acted in a manner that appeared to him best under the circumstances, and he boldly defends his cause, well knowing that many will take exception to it. Whilst we admire his candour, as well as his personal courage, we must respectfully protest against his conception of missionary duty, and we rejoice to see that the Wesleyan Board of Missions has passed a resolution in the most considerate terms in which a censure could be conveyed. To other Polynesia missions it has been the rule that when the danger of murder became so great that teachers could not be asked to risk it, they should be withdrawn to some spot where they could wait the turn of events and the providential openings which mark such undertakings. When withdrawal has not been practicable, the teachers and Christian natives have been gathered together and have assumed an attitude of defence. In Mr. Brown's narrative we see nothing to justify the departure from these almost sacred traditions of missionary work, and we sincerely hope no other missionaries or native teachers will follow his example, for we look upon the men of peace scattered throughout the Southern Seas as pioneers of commerce, civilization, and religion, whose influence will be quite different in kind if it is thought that they may be transferred into warlike leaders if sufficiently provoked.'

"But our contemporary is in error, we think, in its interpretation of the resolutions of the Board of Missions—Mr. Brown was not censured. For the rest the letter of the general secretary in our last issue shows how impracticable was the idea of withdrawal.

"The *Echo* regards the finding of the Board of Missions as ' cautious, in fact, a sort of open verdict.' It speaks of the New Britain natives as a compound of the simplicity which is childish and the ferocity which is devilish, and remarks that the effort to lift a people from such unspeakable brutishness is one at which most of us can only wonder. Mr. Brown's defence must rest on the supposition that the mission party and the traders were in imminent danger, and is put thus: 'If the rest of the teachers and their families, if Mr. Brown's own family, and if the traders scattered among the islands, were in danger of becoming the victims of a horde of savages, who, fresh from one cannibal feast, were longing for a more sumptuous one, then what Englishman, what Australian, would blame him, who was a man as well as a missionary, for defending all the lives which were threatened? The plots for the murder of the widows and children of the slain teachers, and for the slaughter of the other teachers and their families; the evident belief of the traders, that their lives were in great danger; the general insolent and clamorous temper of heathens, hitherto friendly; the abduction of a teacher's wife by the chief of the town, and the message sent to Mr. Brown, that the taro was ready with which to eat him—all this was enough to make an ordinary European, even though a Christian, think that the time for gunpowder had come, as well as the time for prayer.' But the *Echo* adds: 'We must add, however, that it is no part of missionary duty to retaliate, and that violence was justifiable only so far as it was essential to immediate self-defence and personal safety, and even then it is a question whether safety should not have been sought by avoiding conflict rather than by aggression. It is not right that any man or body of men should usurp the functions of Her Majesty's High Commissioner for Polynesia. Sir Arthur Gordon is the High Commissioner, but is at present in England, having recently obtained leave of absence. We hear that Chief Justice Gorrie of Fiji is Sir Arthur Gordon's deputy. and it may be presumed that prompt inquiry will be made into the affair.'

"The *Australian Witness*, organ of the Presbyterian Church in New South Wales, thus refers to the expedition against the inland natives. Such procedure has often been the means of checking the wild savages of hill tribes in the South Sea Islands. But many will question the action of Mr. Brown as a missionary in this slaughter. A High Commissioner, the Governor of Fiji, has been appointed to deal with all such cases. And even the commodore has to respect his authority. If Mr. Brown could have waited for the High Commissioner or his deputy to take action, no doubt he would gladly have protected his own missionary reputation from the peril to which it is now exposed, but how could he tarry? The danger was immediate, while on the other hand the intelligence has only just reached the Deputy High Commissioner in Fiji.' The *Australian Witness* adds: 'The Gospel has turned the savage people in Fiji, and some of the converts have become first-rate teachers and missionaries to other islands.

"'It is this influence alone which can bring the other savage races of Polynesia into civilization; Christianity has invariably been the civilizing process in the South Seas. It is not at all likely that the mission will be given up because of this disaster.

"'The blood of the martyrs will in New Britain, as in Old Britain and other lands, become the seed of the Church.'

"The *Queensland Evangelical Standard* epitomises the narrative which appeared in these columns, but does not commit itself to any decided criticism.

"It says: 'Opinions will differ among friends and

foes as to the propriety of the action taken by the avengers (?). Persons at a distance, who have had no dealings with treacherous savages, can have but a faint idea of the great peril the foreigners were in.'

"The *Southern Cross*, an unsectarian Protestant paper published in Melbourne, observes: 'It is deeply to be deplored that blood has been shed, and we are not surprised to read that great diversity of opinion exists as to the course adopted by the Rev. George Brown. The affair has an ugly look, but we feel sure that we have not all the facts of the case before us. Fuller information may give it quite a different complexion, and meanwhile it is better to suspend judgment. Past experience has taught us to be cautious how we receive the first accounts that reach us of alleged aggression and violence on the part of Christian missionaries.'

"The *Spectator*, Melbourne, says: 'While we must regret that it was deemed necessary for the protection of the white men and native teachers to inflict severe punishment even on cruel and treacherous cannibals, no one but Mr. Brown and those who took the lead in the expedition are capable of estimating the nature of the emergency, and the fact that a brave but humane and good man should have deemed himself justified in taking up arms against the murderers, is at least *primâ facie* evidence that he acted for the best.'

"'X. Y. Z.,' a constant contributor to the *Spectator*, with characteristic outspokenness, writes: 'Mr. Brown's relation to his teachers was peculiar. He had led them into peril—it was in response to his call they had left their native islands and sailed over strange seas to death. And when the men had fallen was their leader to look calmly on and let their wives and little ones perish under the club of the cannibal? Let us translate the case into terms we can better understand. Suppose some midnight the Mission Secretary of Sydney discovered an assassin in his house bent on taking his children's lives. It is certain that on the highest Christian principles he would knock the ruffian down, and if no gentler dissuasive were sufficient to shelter the lives dependent upon him, would knock the man's brains out. It would, no doubt, be a distressing and shocking necessity; and it seems to have been a necessity not less sharp and tragic which spurred Mr. Brown to action. Perhaps when all the facts are known it may be possible to dissent from this reading of the necessities of the case, but it is unfair and ungenerous to condemn him before the full facts are known.'

"One other Press criticism we notice—it is that of the *Melbourne Age*. Flippant, palpably unjust comment might be expected from some insignificant prints in the colonies. There are papers without a shred of moral character, scandals to journalistic literature, pandering to infidelity and lust, and that they should attack Mr. Brown might grieve those who appreciate a self-sacrificing life, but could not possibly excite surprise.

"The *Age*, however, enjoys a very large circulation,

and is understood to be the organ of the dominant
political party in Victoria; it is therefore astonish-
ing to find in its columns a sub-leader which, for
flippancy of style and prejudiced distortion of facts,
could hardly be surpassed. This precious deliver-
ance is thus perorated: 'If Wesleyan Christianity
obtains a foothold in New Britain it will have been
by the means introduced by Mohammed—the sword
in one hand, the book in the other—baptism or
butchery, the only alternative of the people.' The
Rev. John Watsford replied to the *Age* in just
such a manly letter as might have been expected
from him, in the course of which he says: 'I do not
complain that you condemn Mr. Brown's conduct,
but I do most earnestly protest against the way in
which you have done this. For the murderers you
can find some excuse, some pity, but for the missionary none. Surely Mr. Brown's character, his noble
work, and the peculiarly trying and dangerous
position in which he was placed, demand some
consideration, and should lead those who blame him
to do so as tenderly and mercifully as the circumstances of the case will warrant.' After narrating
Mr. Brown's services in the cause of humanity, and
recounting the difficult circumstances in which he was
placed in New Britain, Mr. Watsford thus concludes:
'The *Age* might have shown some consideration for
the committee so sorely tried by these painful events.
That it has not done so has not surprised us, for the
Wesleyan Church has learned to expect from certain
quarters but little commendation for the good it

does, and no mercy for the mistakes it makes.'   We
only wish to add in this connection, that the exten-
sive Press criticism (of which the foregoing is but a
part) which has followed the news of the defensive
measures adopted by the mission party in New
Britain, cannot fail to produce one result; it will
impress upon missionaries—if such impression should
be necessary—that force should be resorted to with
infinite reluctance, and can be justified by nothing
save peril of the most unmistakable and extreme
character."

CHAPTER VII.

I SHALL now try and describe some of the arms and implements of the New Britain natives in the district of Kininigunun and Blanche Bay.

First in importance are the tomahawks, the heads of which used to be formerly entirely of stone, but since the white trader has come to this part of the island it has been much given up for the iron head. The stone heads were wedged between two pieces of wood, much in the same manner as those in New Guinea, but not so nicely finished, and the handle was also longer and more awkward. But with the iron-head tomahawk they fasten it on to a long handle highly ornamented, and the head is kept well greased with candle-nut oil, as is also the staff of the handle; notches are cut just below the head to show the number of victims that have fallen by the hand of the owner. Next in importance are the clubs. These are of several kinds; the most common are made of wood, in the shape of a somewhat elongated constable's staff. Another kind have a curious head of a conical shape—these are decorated

with different colours, red, white, and blue, with
strings of beads fastened to the handle. The stone
club is the most formidable weapon of the kind that
I have ever seen—it is formed by a large round

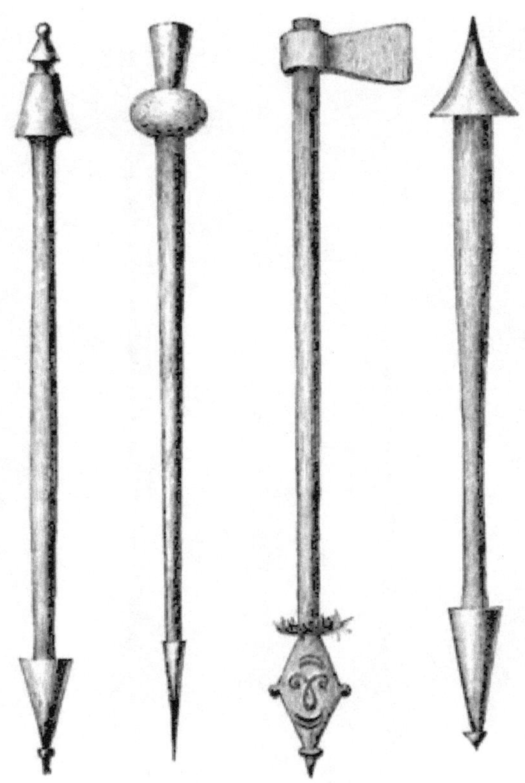

STONE CLUBS AND HATCHET, NEW BRITAIN.

ball of stone on one end and with a long wooden
handle through a hole in its centre.

The way it is made is peculiar : the native first
takes a piece of suitable granite which he places in a
slow fire of cocoa-nut shells, which give an immense

heat, and allows it to become red hot. He then, by the aid of a split bamboo in the place of tongs, removes it from the fire, and begins to drop water on it drop by drop, each drop falling exactly on the same place.

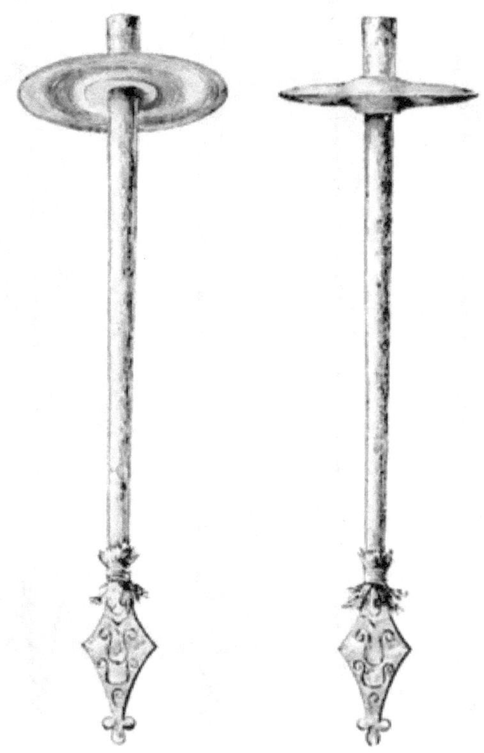

That portion of the stone on which the water falls begins to fly and crack off, until the heat has gone out of the stone. He then repeats the operation until an irregular hole is formed through the centre; he then fixes a stick through it, and takes it off to a place where there is a large granite rock in which is a dent like a small basin.

He hits the stone upon the rock until all the rough corners are knocked off and it is worn fairly round ; then takes the end of the stick, and pressing the stone down into the hollow of the rock makes the stick revolve rapidly between his hands, weighting it with other stones fastened to the top of the stick, until that side of the stone is worn perfectly smooth and round. He then shifts the other side of the stone downwards and works at that until both are smooth and even, choosing a handle of tough wood, about four feet long, on to which he fixes the stone with gum from the bread-fruit tree, leaving about four inches protruding at one end beyond the stone.

One club that I bought had a flat circular stone beautifully made and of the size of an ordinary china plate, with a sharp edge on the circumference. There are only certain natives who can make these stone clubs, for which they obtain high prices.

The sling is also a weapon that these natives use with great accuracy and force. It is formed of two long strings, each of which is about two feet six inches in length, one having a pearl-shell button fastened to the end; this is to prevent its slipping through the fingers, whilst the other string is finished off to a taper point. These two strings are joined together by a flat piece of bark of the cocoa-nut tree (usually) which is the receptacles for the stone. On throwing, the two ends of the string are held in the right hand, the button being between the second and third fingers, the stone resting on the piece of bark is swung rapidly round and round the head with the right arm bent, and when sufficient impetus has been given, the pointed end of the string is let go, and the stone flies, the string at the same time cracking like a whip.

I have seen a native knock a bird off a tree at about one hundred yards distant; they seldom pitch the stone further from an object aimed at than three or four yards.

The spears are of various kinds—some, and these the most commonly used, are made from the hard outside bark of the cocoa-nut palms; they are quite plain and rough, only having the sharp point burnt in the fire a little in order to harden it.

Others are made of tau-wood, which is very tough; others from a bastard ebony that grows in these islands—they are generally plain.

The spears they use for "close quarters" mostly have a shin or arm-bone stuck on to the butt end. These bones are those of some enemy killed in fighting, as they attach superstitious value to them, supposing them to give the throwing power of the man to whom the bones belonged in addition to their own.

The spears used for festive occasions are decorated with a large conical-shaped arrangement of feathers, very artistically worked, blue, green, red and white being the usual colours. The feathers are obtained

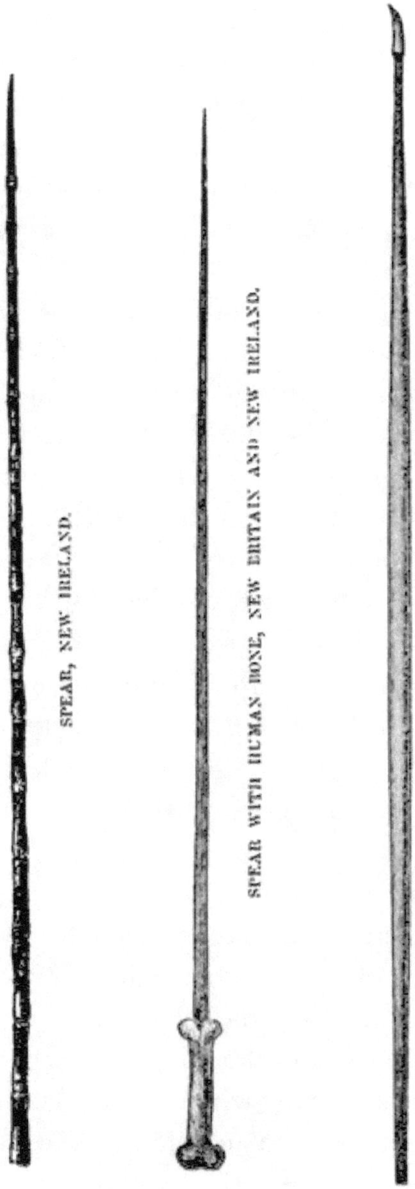

SPEAR, NEW IRELAND.

SPEAR WITH HUMAN BONE, NEW BRITAIN AND NEW IRELAND.

SPEAR WITH CASSOWARY'S CLAW TIP, SPACIOUS BAY, NEW BRITAIN.

from the gay-plumaged parrots that abound in these islands. Their clubs used in the dances are also decorated in the same manner. In some of their dances they use a " Marlargen " in each hand ; these are thin pieces of wood with the figures of men or animals carved on them, and being so light and thin, they bend and shake with each movement of the dancer.

These natives have also a curious idea that the skull after death is the place to which the spirit of the departed person resorts when it returns from its journeyings, and for this reason they use the skulls of their departed friends in dancing. The method is this, they cut the skulls in half, taking away any small bones or other matter from the inside of the face half of the skull, which on the outside they fill up in the original form with gum, lime, &c., to represent the face of the human being as nearly as possible. Across the back of the lower jawbone they fix a piece of wood, which is held in the mouth of the person that is dancing ; these masks are used in the " toberran " dances elsewhere described.

The surgical instruments used by these natives are a piece of obsidian, a shark's tooth, and if obtainable a piece of glass bottle.

In the case of a broken leg or arm the flesh is cut open to the bone, which is drawn into position and a piece of bamboo inserted next to the bone to keep it in its place, and the wound is then bound up.

After the bone has set the bamboo works out

through the opening that was made, and the wound is then allowed to heal. I have seen men that have undergone this operation and they walked with ease. I have also seen a man that had new teeth put in made of pearl-shell. This was accomplished in the following manner : the gums in the place where the teeth were required were cut lengthways down to the bone, then a piece of pearl-shell was inserted of the required size which rested on the bone, the gums were then allowed to grow back into their place, being held by a little arrangement made of bamboo, which pressed them together, the man in the meantime being fed on soft food so as not to disturb the healing. They bleed for every conceivable ailment, cutting that part affected. If a man has a headache they will tie a tight band round the head across the forehead, and then cut deep gashes into the skin until the blood flows freely. When sufficient has been taken away they stop the bleeding with burnt lime. It is a common thing to see a man with his face, chest, arms, legs, and stomach covered with the marks of the surgical bleeding-instrument.

The surgeons are also magicians or wind and rain makers ; they pretend to be able to cure anything, or make any one ill, however distant that person may be ; also that they control the wind and rain. I saw a very peculiar cure performed by one of these wind-makers or doctors, which tends to show how much trickery there is made up with what is real in their practice, and also what a great help faith is in sickness. I wanted a man to go with me in a canoe to a place some distance off. When I got to his house, his " woman " told me he was sick, and could not go. "Oh," I said, " I will give him a good big present if he will come, besides paying for the hire of the canoe." "Well," she said, "will you pay the doctor for him? then he may be able to go." I consented, and the doctor was sent for. The man came out of his house looking indeed wretchedly ill. I felt his pulse, looked at his tongue, and he appeared to me to be suffering from a description of fever. On his arrival the doctor first asked him what he felt; he told him and the doctor then said, "Oh, yes, there are two worms in your stomach, I can see them, I will take them away and you will be all right." The doctor then made the man stand up with his hands over his head, and waved some sprigs of ginger-plant about him, the meanwhile singing a sort of chant; after this he took some burnt lime in the hollow of his hand and blew it against the man's stomach three times; he then began to scratch the man's navel with one finger, gradually approaching his mouth to the patient's stomach and drawing in his breath. The woman then supplied him with half a cocoa-nut shell full of water, which he took in his left hand, placing his mouth close to the man's navel, drew back suddenly and began retching violently over the cocoa-nut shell. Presently a large worm dropped out of his mouth. The doctor did all this a second time with the same result, and then told the man he was cured. The man went with me to the place I wished, paddling the whole way there and back—a distance of some thirty miles.

I looked at the worms, they were unlike any I had seen before, and appeared as if they certainly might have come from a man's body.

One of the native boys, who had accompanied me to the man's house, and to whom I had expressed

NEW BRITAIN CANOE, GAZELLE PENINSULA.

my opinion that the doctor was a humbug, turned round to me and said, "There, do you call that gammon?" It certainly was a very clever bit of imposition, but it had the desired effect.

In the case of a chief wishing to make a trading voyage in his canoes, he generally first consults one of these wind-makers, and pays him to make the weather fine. Of course it is part of these men's business to be thoroughly conversant with the changes of the weather, and if they see that it is likely to be adverse they plead all manner of excuses. They sometimes say that another chief is going the opposite way, and that they cannot change the direction of the wind until his journey is over. This is but one of the many excuses they make use of in order to put off their dupes.

If, however, they see the weather is likely to be fair, then they make the best bargain they can with the chief who is wishing to start; but of course, should the weather turn out bad during this journey, they put it down to the want of payment.

They are very sharp, clever men, these wind-makers; indeed, were they not they would soon lose their custom, and as likely as not get a spear through them as well.

When pretending to make the wind blow in the right direction they take burnt lime in their hands, and throw it up in the air singing a sort of chant all the time. They then wave sprigs of ginger and other plants about, throwing them up and catching them. At the last they make a small fire with these sprigs on the spot where the lime has fallen thickest to the ground, walking round the fire chanting a few notes repeatedly, but in a low tone. They then take the ashes and throw them on the water, and the ceremony is complete.

To any one who was a casual observer of these natives it would appear that they were trying to propitiate some god or performing a rite of worship; but in reality it is not so, but simply that these clever rogues know how easily their fellow-natives are impressed by outward ceremonial, and when they see all this going on, and find that the result is as they wished it to be, of course these simple savages put it down to the wind-maker having a super-natural power, or at all events one superior to their own. This is the result the doctor wishes to obtain in order to establish his reputation, and therefore nothing can be done by these men without a great deal of outward show.

Of the religion of these natives it is hard to speak with assurance, as there appears at first sight to be no positive law, order, or even similar ideas in any two places.

The real fact is that they have no knowledge of any God, that is to say, one to be worshipped. They have a belief in a superior being, that originally formed the land on which they live, but it is always spoken of as a being that was at a very remote period, not one that is now, in existence.

I have heard some declare that it was a huge pig that rooted the earth up and formed the mountains and valleys. ·

The natives are very superstitious regarding the spirits of their departed friends or enemies, which they consider have either a bad or good influence as the case may be.

In conversation one day with an old man about the spirits of the deceased he told me that the stars were lamps hung by the departed spirits to light the way for those that should come after ; where he did not say, and although I questioned him closely on the subject, he had no ideas as to the sort of place that it is they come to at last. He only knew that the spirit went across the water to the moon at rising, and getting into her was carried to the region of the stars, from whence they returned to visit the earth by the same means.

I tried to puzzle him by asking him how it was that the moon was sometimes large and sometimes small; he replied that when it was small there were not so many spirits requiring to go, as it was always at the full moon that most people died, and that was always the time when most spirits required to visit the earth.

They are terribly afraid of an eclipse as being something far beyond their comprehension, indeed they cannot account for it except by the wild notion that the spirits are angry.

I had a native on board at one time who was suddenly seized with fever, though he said that some one of his enemies had bewitched him. This, he explained to me, had been done by obtaining some banana skins of which he had eaten the fruit, and making magic over them and then burning them. This is the reason that these natives are always careful to hide or burn the refuse of anything that they have been eating, for by this means they declare it is possible to make your enemy ill, or even to die. In the case of the young man in question I determined to try a little simple magic myself, as this appears to be the best and only manner of dealing with these natives when they get this idea into their head. I therefore agreed with him, and told him I could drive the evil out of him, as white men understood far more *real* magic than his people. I told him to stand forward by the foremast and look at a penny which I placed in his hand—that was in reality to gain time.

I went below into the cabin and fastened a long string to the starting catch of a large musical box I had. I then went to my medicine chest, and mixed a strong dose of quinine and brandy; I also took out a spoonful of flour of sulphur, which I placed in a glass tube.

These I then took on deck as well as the string attached to the musical box, which I concealed on one side of the skylight. Then I called the man aft, and told him to open his mouth and shut his eyes (as one does to children), and I blew the sulphur down his throat. This nearly choked him, but I knew it must be something severe or he would not believe in my magic. I walked round him a little, and then gave him the quinine and brandy; I then told him to lie down on the deck, and if he heard a "toberran" singing he would be perfectly cured. Without moving from where I stood, I pulled the string and the box began to play; in the meantime the native was extremely agitated, and when the music began he shouted and screamed with excitement.

I would not allow him to run away as he wanted to, but made him lie down on a mat on the deck, and soon the brandy began to affect him, and he fell asleep, to wake up quite cured. But it had rather an unfortunate result, for he sounded my praises so much amongst other natives that I found myself inundated with patients to such an extent that I had to refuse any more medical aid.

These natives have very diverse laws with regard to their feeding. In Kininigunun the women are tabooed from eating any pig or tortoise; in Karavia the men are tabooed from eating anything but human flesh, fowls, or fish; this is also the case in Nodup, or was before cannibalism was supposed to be stopped.

The natives are extremely fond of dogs' flesh, but this only on rare occasions that one is cooked, most generally on the occasion of the death of a chief, when a feast is made by his successor.

The flesh of young alligators is also considered a great delicacy; the cassowary, wallaby, and magapode are eaten; fowls' eggs are very numerous, as also in some parts are those of the magapode—these latter are very rich.

Cassowaries' eggs are generally blown before being eaten, as the shell is much prized as an ornament. Turtles' eggs are consumed in large quantities both raw and cooked. There is a large description of spider that is considered a very delicate article of food. They take off the legs and place the bodies in a half cocoa-nut shell over a fire, and when thoroughly warmed they eat them.

They eat every kind of bird they can catch, as

well as flying foxes, flying squirrels, and bats; yams, taro, and sweet potatoes form their staple vegetable, but they also cook the leaves of the taro and sweet potato. Bananas are seldom eaten ripe, as they generally pick them quite green, and say they are more wholesome cooked in this state than if eaten ripe; bread-fruit and jack-fruit are also very commonly eaten by these natives.

Their method of cooking is to make a hole in the ground and light a fire in it, into this is dropped a number of hard stones that become red hot. Should it be a pig that they intend cooking, some of these stones are taken out by a pair of bamboo tongs and placed inside the carcase, subsequent to its having been singed over a grass fire and cleaned; it is then wrapped in banana leaves, placed in the hole and covered with the remainder of the stones, and is finally all covered in with banana leaves and heaped up with earth; this is left for about two hours, when it is taken out and the skin is divided into little squares with a sharp shell or piece of obsidian.

Every other article of food is treated in the same manner, as they have no vessels in which to boil. The natives make a kind of cake of the flour obtained from the kernel of the " tan "-fruit, and also from crushed "tunups" or wild almonds. They smoke pigs' flesh for keeping, as well as some kinds of fish. Salt is never used in their food, nor do they seem to have an idea that it is necessary, except as medicine; for this it is much prized by the inland or bush people, who buy cocoa-nut shells and bamboo bottles full of salt-water from the shore tribes.

They eat all manner of shell-fish, and most of the sea fish and eels, but there are some kinds that they consider as very poisonous, and undoubtedly they are so, as I have seen some of my men very ill from eating a fish that was stated to be poisonous by a native of the place.

Squid or cuttle-fish is a delicacy they are fond of, hammering them well with a heavy stone before cooking, which is done in banana leaves, with cocoa-nut milk added, which gives it a most delicious flavour.

There is in these islands a small bee that makes a honey tasting much like raspberry vinegar, and is considered a great luxury by the people. The cooking is on the whole very good, and I must say I like most of the native dishes, and think good taro is the best vegetable of the kind I ever tasted.

In fishing, these natives use beautifully made fish-traps, as well as the rod and net (as before described). These traps are moored with a rope made of cane twisted together attached to a stone. This kind of fishing is practised sometimes in very great depths of water, even as much as one hundred fathoms. This fish-trap is made of plaited cane, very neatly worked in pattern something like the seat of a cane chair, and is oblong in form, open at both ends, with a number of slight canes converging from the opening to the centre, where a space is left for the fish to get into the pot; but these canes being pointed, they on trying to return are met by the points, and so cannot get out.

Another mode of catching fish is with a number of prickly palm branches, which are all tied together at one end and worked round with fibre so as to form a cone with the hooked thorns pointing inwards towards the apex, where a piece of bait is fixed. A bit of light wood is fastened to the trap with

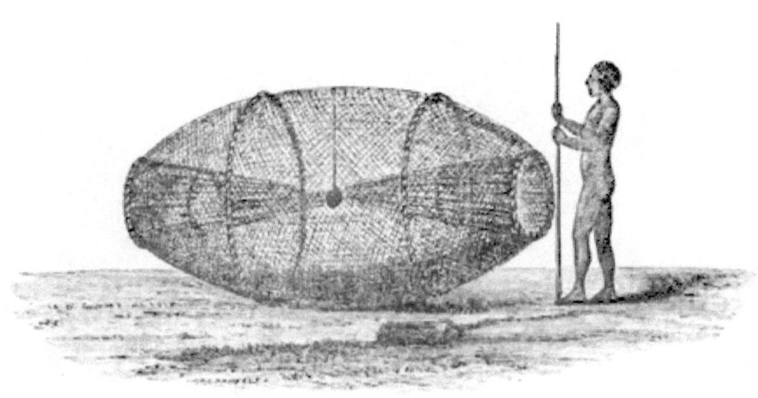

WOOP OR FISHING-BASKET, NEW BRITAIN.

a long string. With this trap the native dives and places it on the edge of a reef, putting a stone on the string near it, so that the wood will float on the water whilst the trap remains below. The fish seeing the bait makes a rush for it, and gets his head into the trap, without any difficulty, but when he tries to back out he finds himself hooked on all sides, and in his frantic endeavours to get clear pulls the string from under the stone, and the native, seeing the piece of wood moving, jumps into the water and tows it to shore.

The hooks for lines are made of tortoise-shell, and the bait for spinning is formed of pearl-shell in the shape of a fish, having a tortoise-shell hook on the tail. They also use a spear with five points, four on the outside and one in the middle.

There is a description of creeper which, when bruised and thrown into the water, the fish eat and

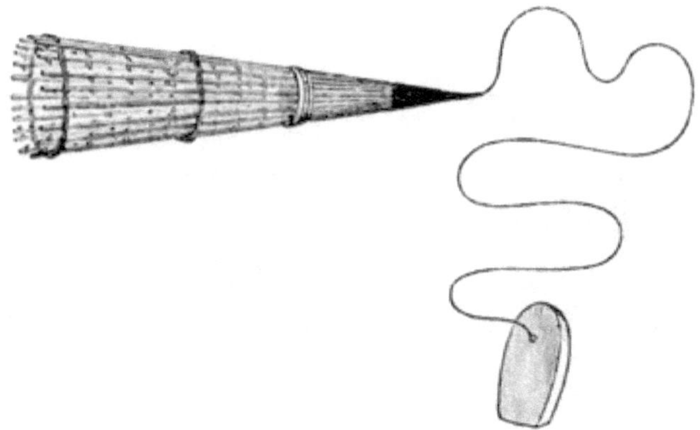

FISH TRAP, MADE OF PRICKLY PALM, NEW BRITAIN.

appear to become intoxicated, for they turn up and become quite helpless, when they fall an easy prey to the native.

The houses of these natives are as a general rule not of a very high order, being often only small huts made of bamboo and thatched with either grass or sugar-cane leaves. For each village two large houses are built, one for the men, the other for the women. No man is allowed in the women's house, nor is any woman allowed in the men's house; the latter is generally used for a council house. They are lined with bunks made of bamboo which extend along both sides of the house, serving either as beds or seats.

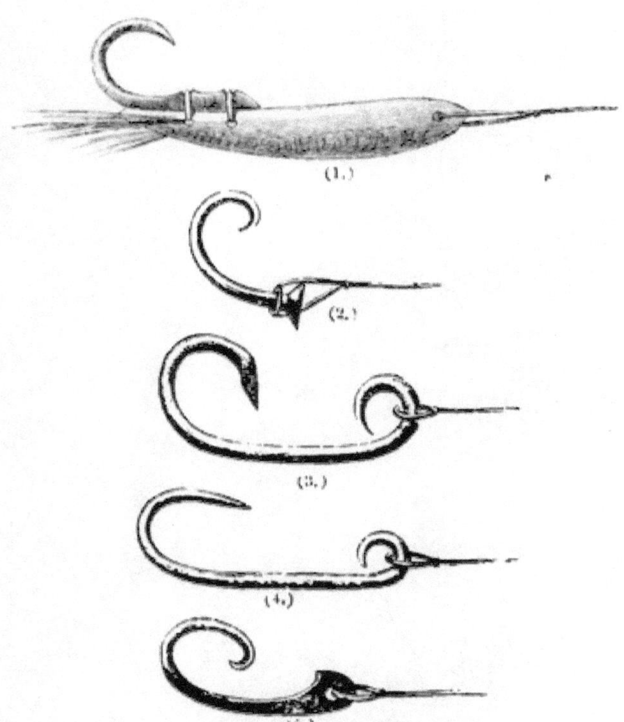

(1.) Spinning pearl-shell bait.   (2.) Hook made from iron nail.
(3.) Tortoise-shell hook.   (4.) Tortoise-shell hook.   (5.) Clam-shell hook.

FISHING HOOKS FROM NEW BRITAIN.

These houses are generally built in the form of an ellipse, the eaves of the thatch coming down to within three feet of the ground, but inside the walls are six feet high, over which the roof arches to about eighteen feet. The inside is carefully blackened with

VILLAGE, NEW BRITAIN (GAZELLE PENINSULA).

To face page 13.

the smoke of cocoa-nut shells, which forms a description of enamel, and does not rub off; it also (the natives assured me) preserves the rafters and timbers from rot and worm. The outside enclosure is planted generally with variegated plants and the ground is kept beautifully clean; the whole being enclosed by a fence of bamboo.

Opposite the chief's house is generally the taboo tree, decorated with the lower jawbones of pigs, which are hung in profusion all over it. It is on this tree that the unfortunate victims of cannibalism are despatched and their bodies exposed for sale; it is generally painted with red and white bands as well as with representations of faces.

CHAPTER VIII.

THUS far what I have written applies only to the east and a portion of the north coast from Return Point to Kabakadaie in New Britain, and to Duke of York Island. I will now ask the reader to accompany me into the western and hitherto unexplored part of New Britain lying between Cape Lambert, the northern point, and Cape Gloucester, the easternmost point of this island. From Cape Stephens westward along the coast of Goonan and Ruterwool districts, which terminate in Tarlily Bay, are groves of cocoa-nut palms interspersed with the foliage of other fruit-bearing trees, such as the bread-fruit, banana, and tumup, whilst further inland are seen the tops of the elegant betel-nut palm waving above the less lofty greenwood and fey-fey trees, at the back rising the volcanic upheavals of probably thousands of years covered with grass that in the distance looks soft and velvety, but in reality is higher than a man's head, in many cases coarse and thorny.

It is strange that the custom of the Duk-duk is not practised in Ruterwool, although it is in full operation amongst the tribes surrounding it. I have never found any reason for this, which is certainly a very curious fact.

Tarlily Bay is surrounded by comparatively low land, with large plantations of bananas flourishing close to the shore; inland, at a distance of about two miles, the hills spring up to a considerable altitude. This bay is named after that chief who caused so much trouble to Mr. Brown, as I have already described.

This man was certainly the most cunning, at the same time one of the most fearless, chiefs I met with on this island. He was constantly on board my little vessel whilst she was anchored in this bay. He appeared to be confident that I would not take any mean advantage of him, although I had been very active against him in the late fighting, and might at any moment have made him a prisoner; indeed he at last went so far as to promise me that he would go to see Mr. Brown at Duke of York with me on my promising that no harm should befall him. However, I never had a chance of taking him, I am sorry to say. He is small in stature and covered with buckwar, and is altogether a very ugly man, but his eyes are quick, piercing, and very intelligent. I believe that

although he is cunning, cruel, and a cannibal, it is
solely from want of better knowledge, or rather
perhaps I should say from force of habit.

Junior Mission House Point is the north-eastern
point of Kabakadaie, and is now distinguished by a
mission-house that has lately been erected here for
the residence of the Junior White Missionary. It is
rather a warm corner for him though, having Tarlily
on one side and a chief called Bulilie on the other,
who is anything but a true friend of the mission.
This point on Tarlily Bay side falls abruptly to
the beach in a cliff of about forty feet drop;
on the north-western side it is more shelving,
but has moderately steep hills at the back. There
is a considerable fringe reef lying from it about a
quarter of a mile, inside of which there is a boat
passage; this reef extends along the whole of
Kabakadaie, which is the next district, and is
fronted by a long, nearly straight piece of coast
running in a west-south-westerly direction to Shoal
Point. There is a good anchorage off the reef,
the depth of water varying from six to twenty
fathoms. It is a very lovely piece of coast with its
many groves of palms and surrounding villages of
more or less importance, whilst at the back are seen
rising lofty hills, dotted here and there with many-
coloured shrubs and trees ; on the beach are a number
of canoes and long lengths of " cudda " or cane
ropes, with the " woop " or fish-traps to which they
are attached to moor them in deep water.

Every here and there is seen the peculiar fence

painted in fantastic patterns to denote the taboo ground of the Duk-duk, inside which fence is invariably seen the house of this gentleman, where he is supposed to reside ; and at times one may see strange figures dancing along the beach and uttering those peculiar cries that give notice of his approach, whilst at another spot in an open space are a crowd of small boys engaged in a sham fight.

Sides having been formed, each of them proceeds to collect as many of the green fruit of a tree that grows on the shore as they can, having already provided themselves with long green reeds that grow on swampy ground. When sufficient ammunition has been collected the mimic fight begins ; the green seeds are used in slings, and the reeds are for spears, both of which are thrown with great accuracy by these embryo warriors, who often have an old man acting as instructor and umpire. These fights are kept up with great spirit for hours together, and by this means the lads are trained to the use of their native arms, and some become great experts in the use of one or the other weapon, if not both. It is a great disgrace to be taken prisoner, and therefore it is practice to them in running as well as the use of arms. I have seen some very nasty blows given by the seeds used in the slings, but as they have only been considered a laughing matter by the others I suppose nothing much was thought of such trifles.

Further on will perhaps be seen a group of children of both sexes engaged in making little oval cakes of sand in their hands and throwing them up into the air to fall into the water ; if they break it is not considered to count as one to the thrower. The game consists in seeing how many can be thrown without breaking, and the higher the more success ; if they drop whole into the water, they do so with a hollow sound that always determines the mark. As each one drops in whole the player makes a mark on the sand with his foot to enable him to remember how often he succeeds running ; if one breaks he has to rub out and begin afresh. I have often seen grown men and women playing at this game, and have tried to throw them myself, but found it no easy matter to do so successfully ; they appear very fond of it, and will keep it up all day.

Sometimes, too, may be seen a long line of women tramping along with their heavy loads to market, some with baskets full of yams, others with taro, cocoa-nuts, &c., strapped on to their backs and across the forehead. Perhaps on the top of the baskets on some woman's back will be a network bag containing her latest olive branch, either sleeping in perfect comfort or taking refreshment in the most stoical manner possible ; here and there are men and boys running and playing in the water. I have seen little children that could hardly walk when on shore swim like little fish as soon as their legs were off the bottom—they seem to take to it like water-spaniels. On calm days some boys will sail their toy canoes, and beautiful little models they often are, though others seem to be just as pleased with half a cocoa-nut husk, in which they fix an upright stick with a leaf on it to represent a sail, and this seems somewhat curious as both in New Britain and New Ireland they have no proper sails to their canoes—just a mat on a pole for going before the wind. I suppose the idea must come from the vessels that they have seen passing their shores.

Altogether it is a most animated sight, and looking at it and hearing the merry peals of laughter that ring out from the shore, it does seem hard to realize that perhaps to-morrow some of them will be engaged in torturing some poor wretch that has fallen into their hands and afterwards in eating him. It is a most unpleasant thought to come at such a time of apparent happiness and innocence, yet it is, alas, too true that here, where nature seems to have expended her greatest art in rendering the earth beautiful, where her lavish hand has spared nothing to render these islands most exquisite, here her most perfect work *man* is the one thing evil and debased.

On our way to Port Webber we passed Midway Reef, that lies almost mid-channel between Shoal Point and Man Island: it shows a-wash at low water. Next comes Luin Bay, a pretty fair anchorage for small vessels during the south-east monsoon. A valley runs back from Luin Bay, formed by the Kabakadaie Hills on one side and Luin Hills on the other; it is a pretty open piece of country, and would form a good spot for sugar-cane growing, I should fancy, were there any mills in this part of the world to crush the cane when grown. However, it will be many years, I suppose, before agriculture of that kind is carried on here. Next comes Cape Luin with an immense reef running from it about a mile in extent. Luin itself is high and thinly covered with trees; several fishing villages may be seen on the shore on the other side of the reef.

Between this reef and the Island of Urara is the passage that takes us into Port Webber. Now we round the extreme edge of the reef and run along the shore, the reef gradually getting smaller and smaller, and as the last of it loses itself on shore we sight the noble mountain of Beautemps Beaupré, which serves as a good landmark to steer for, as running up for it will take us into a good anchorage, clear of the fringe reefs off the Cambira coast. This anchorage to which we are now steering appears to be the only one for vessels of any size in Port Webber; it is sheltered from the south-east monsoon, but the north-west blows directly into it, though it is seldom that much sea gets up inside, owing to the numerous reefs which surround the mouth of the port.

Port Webber is a deep embayment about six miles long, and with the south-east monsoon is almost like an inland sea, it is so smooth and calm. On the eastern side it is formed, as we have before stated, by the shore of Luin district, but the head of the bay is a district called Cambira. This is fairly populated, and a good many villages show themselves amongst the thick foliage along the shore, but the main part of the inhabitants have dwellings on the high grassy hills about two miles from the beach, above which towers Mount Beautemps Beaupré to the height of about one thousand eight hundred feet. Several small streams gush out from under the bushes and plough their way through the sand to the sea. Here I landed, and wishing to go some distance inland obtained the guidance of the old chief of the district (I forget his name, but it was a very long one). We started off through the bush, a party of about ten, natives leading. The shore was belted with scrub for some little distance, and then gradually merged into grassy plain land; the grass is very high in some places, quite two feet above our heads, though the tracks are quite clear, but they are only about two feet wide. How easy it would be for these natives to form an ambush in the high grass did they intend any treachery; a spear could be launched at one without your being able to see where the thrower was in the least.

In some places the grass had been burnt in patches to make way for yam planting. All my guides were armed with different weapons, some with the common wooden spear, others with trade tomahawks (though not many of those), and one had a kind of sword made from the outside wood of the cocoa-nut or betel-nut palm, and cut with jagged teeth something like a saw, with which they beat back any stray bushes or grass in the track; one man had a club something the shape of a spade without the shoulders. These I saw many of afterwards: they generally have the end of the handle covered with net-work, sometimes stained with different colours, but generally whitened with " ker-bung " or lime ; the broad end is concave, with a half-moon shaped ornament on either side ; the chief had a long-handled comb stuck in his hair, which is common to nearly all the different tribes on the north end of the island ; one or two had stone clubs.

One of the men had lately been made a warrior, and consequently had his breast and stomach tatooed (?), small gashes being cut in the skin in volutes—on the two breasts surrounding the nipples and on the stomach. Into these gashes lime had been rubbed to prevent them bleeding, whilst the front of his body was very handsomely decorated with a red, blue, and white pattern. This poor fellow must have been in great pain from the many gashes; indeed, when stooping he showed how stiff and sore he was by having great difficulty in raising himself again without a groan ; however, the others only laughed at him and seemed to consider it an excellent joke, no doubt having been through it themselves before.

The armlets that these natives wear are composed of finely-plaited grass stained black and yellow, very neatly made with diagonal patterns worked into them. These, I understand, are made by the women, though I never saw any at work on them ; they are worn on the upper part of the arm imme-diately over the biceps. Why they are worn so tight I cannot say, but suppose it is the fashion.

The dialect of these people is much the same as

those of Blanche Bay with a slight difference in the pronunciation.

We shortly got into rising ground, and after traversing a distance of some three miles or thereabouts we found ourselves on the top of one of the grassy hills that appeared over the trees from the head of Port Webber. Here I found the grass cleared away and cocoa-nut trees growing in large clusters about an open space, in which were several houses with a large one in the centre; this large house appeared to be the council or reception house of the chief; in front of it was a large "garamoot" or wooden drum, to be beaten for war or an assembly of any kind. On arriving the chief shouted to some women, and immediately a great bustle commenced, the women hurrying off in all directions. The chief's head woman brought out some mats and placed them in a half circle in front of the large house; she then went into another house, and after we had seated ourselves, myself and the chief in the middle, she returned with a quantity of betel-nut and pepper leaves, and a small bag made of a dried banana leaf full of burnt lime; she handed the betel-nut round to all of us, and then gave the lime-bag to the chief, who courteously handed it to me; but seeing I had some difficulty in getting off the husk of my betel-nut, he took it from me, and putting it into his own mouth, cracked it, and, taking out the kernel, presented it to me. Of course I had to appear pleased and chew away at it with the best grace I could. Soon after the other women came back with cocoa-nuts young and old, of which I was very glad to partake.

We sat and talked a considerable time, he asking many questions as to my country, and also if I would not come and build a house in his district and live with him, he promising for his part to build a house for me and buy me two wives to look after it; for this I was to go fighting with him against his enemies. I did not tell him that I would *not*, and thanked him for his kind offer, but told him that I could not leave my vessel yet, as I had many more people to visit. He held out the advantages of Cambira over any part of his known world (which did not extend more than at most fifty miles away), and did not seem very pleased that I did not jump at so tempting an offer. However, I assured him that when I saw my own people I would tell them what a delightful spot Cambira was, and I had no doubt that some would like to come and live with him. This pacified him somewhat, and he then made me a present of a pig. I told him I would give him a tomahawk and some other things if he would come and see me on board, which he promised to do.

After this he was very civil and conversed in a very friendly manner, and eventually took me to see his taboo (or money), of which he appeared to have a good deal. It was kept in a small hut, in which slept some of his women, and was beautifully packed in coils, covered with split cane netted together, somewhat in the form of a life-belt covered with wicker-work. Each coil contained about two hundred fathoms of this shell-money, and I suppose there were at least four dozen of them laid on mats in this hut. In the case of an attack the women carry them off, and hide or bury them in a pre-arranged spot. We next entered the large hut or council house.

Now I have no ground for saying that it was a council house (as the probabilities are that any council to be held would be in the open air), except that it gave me that idea, as otherwise what use could it have been? Certainly it might have been, as in other parts of New Britain, a young man's sleeping house, but I saw no young men about except those that came with us, and they did not live here, and all the other houses belonged to either the chief's women, his butcher, or his talking man, and their women. It may have been for housing people coming to visit this chief. It was, of course, blackened inside with the smoke of the cocoa-nut shell, as all these natives' houses are, and decorated with the jaw-bones of pigs large and small; a few spears and clubs were stuck up against the wall. It seemed to be about fifty feet long by twenty feet wide, and was also about nine feet high, having two entrances, one on either side. The walls were not more than five feet high, with the thatch overlapping on the outer side and nearly touching the ground. After he had shown me all that he thought would interest me we again sat down on the mats, and then women brought us fowls cooked in banana leaves with cocoa-nut juice and small yams; they also brought us some baked taro and young cocoa-nuts. As

I was very hungry it was to me a most delightful meal.

After this was over we partook of more betel-nut. I then left him, after giving the women all the tobacco I had as well as a few beads, with which they were highly delighted, and, accompanied by some of the men who had guided us up, and who carried the pig slung on a bamboo, I went down to the shore again, and after rewarding them with tobacco returned on board.

The next day the old chief came according to promise, and was much interested in looking over my vessel, and was particularly inquisitive about the little swivel guns; so thinking to please him I loaded one with a blank charge and fired it; he was horribly frightened, and sank back on the deck shaking his head and trying to pull the sound out of his ears. He looked so comical that I began to laugh, and after telling him, " Putta mat " (" No kill anybody "), he seemed much more reassured, but carefully gave the guns a wide berth. He hardly seemed to comprehend my musical box, but held my arm very tight until it had finished playing, then, putting his hand to his mouth, gave vent to the common expression of astonishment of all these natives, " Wo—wo—wo !" I then gave him the promised present, with which he seemed well pleased. We did a good deal of trading with the natives here in yams, fowls' eggs, &c. I had some fun with them about some bad eggs I had bought from one man, which as I was paying for so many things I did not notice until H—— told me they were bad, when taking one in my hand and seeing the native who had sold them to me standing up in his canoe not far off, I threw one at him, saying at the same time, "Picoyina" ("It is bad"). It happened to hit him just in the middle of the forehead, and of course breaking ran down into his eyes and mouth. This so amused the others (and there were a good many there) that they laughed till they cried, and even rolled out of their canoes into the water with laughter. I never saw men in such a condition, they could not forget it, and every now and again would burst out afresh ; it quite stopped my buying anything for some time.

The next day we started off along the western coast of Port Webber towards Materbert Island. On the way we passed a small village built on stakes some distance out into the water, with canoes moored under the houses, very much the same sort of village as one sees in the Gulf of Papua, only not so large ; it is built for fishing, the natives not residing there in the north-west monsoon, as the whole village is liable to be washed away. The coast here is low and swampy, but behind this apparently narrow belt of low land rise the grand volcanic peaks of Byning, rugged and solemn.

Materbert Island seems on approaching it to be part of the mainland, but it is really a rocky islet some quarter of a mile from it, and thickly populated.

The chief's name was "Tobrian," and a good old fellow he was (he died shortly before I left New

Britain), a great friend of mine. The island is a more healthy spot to live on than on the main, though there is also quite a large settlement on the other side of the water, but a river that runs down from the mountains above on this side makes the spot somewhat damp and malarious. I fancy this river contains the coldest water I have felt in any of these streams, and from its being so cold I presume it flows direct from the highest mountains of Byning.

The natives here are a mixture of two races, that of the eastern side of the northern peninsula, and that of the western side, as many of them have that greater regularity of feature and Jewish look that is possessed by the western natives in such a marked degree, that any one seeing them for the first time would immediately notice it, whereas those that we have just left to the east have features less clearly cut and are far more negro-like in appearance. Undoubtedly there are two classes of natives in this island, those that have come from the Solomon Islands and have landed on the eastern and southern sides of it, and those that have come from the north-east coast of New Guinea, and settled on the western and northern sides. It is worthy of note that when Dampier visited Port Montagu he found the people called that land Birara; this name after a considerable interval crops up again just to the northward of Spacious Bay on the east coast. I fancy this goes some way to prove that at one time the south-east and north-east coasts of this island were inhabited by people speaking the same language, and which language is even at the present time somewhat similar to that found in parts of the Solomon group.

In Spacious Bay, where the island is very narrow, are found the same class of natives as those on the western and northern shores, and are identically the same tribes as those found in Open Bay on the north-western side. Whilst I was in these islands a canoe drifted on shore near Gazelle Point with a woman and a boy in it; from what I could gather of the description of the canoe it must have been a Solomon Island one. The woman was killed and eaten, but the boy was kept alive, and I afterwards saw him on board one of Messrs. Godefroy's ships, and judging from his language and appearance he was undoubtedly a Solomon islander, though he seemed to have very confused ideas as to where he had come from.

To resume : these natives of Materbert Island are undoubtedly a mixture of the east and west.

They use the same implements as the natives to eastward, and are great fishers. I have seen beautiful nets made by these people : one that I saw was one hundred and twenty feet in length and seven feet in depth, the sinkers being stones or pieces of coral with holes in them attached to the bottom of the net, whilst the floats were made of pieces of light wood cut into the shape of fish.

Their canoes are large and numerous, some of the larger ones holding as many as twenty natives. When starting for a long trading voyage they are supplied with bamboo buckets as much as six feet in length, with the interior joints broken through except the bottom one ; these are filled with fresh water and are corked with a wisp of banana leaf wound round a stone, which is pressed into a hole in the top joint; they keep the water fresh and cool a long time. They take as provisions baked yams and taro, also some smoked fish. For carrying fire these natives adopt a plan that I have seen elsewhere : they press a quantity of the soft fibrous husk of the ripe cocoanut into a cocoa-nut shell, and then place a red-hot ember in the centre of it; this will smoulder for three or four days, and from it they obtain a light for their cooking fires at any place they may land on the voyage. These natives have also a species of tobacco which they roll up into a rough kind of cigar, and smoke by pressing one end against a lighted fire stick, when they take a long pull, swallowing the smoke and keeping it in the lungs for a considerable time, gradually emitting it from the nose; they seldom take more than one pull at a time, but hand it on to the next man. The leaf much resembles tobacco leaf, but is only allowed to partially dry in the sun, and still retains a green appearance when ready for use ; this when made up has curiously the native name of "Sogar."

Leaving Materbert Island we passed through a narrow passage between a small reef and the mainland, and shortly afterwards came to the island of Matukanaputa ; this is also high, rocky, and thickly populated. These natives are the pirates of the western tribes, as they travel in their canoes along the coast and make raids on the Byning people (who are in reality bushmen, having no canoes and living some distance inland). The Matukanaputa natives are also great turtle fishers, of which they obtain large quantities on the numerous reefs and sand-banks which abound on this part of the coast. They are very similar to the Materbert natives in their habits, but have a stronger affinity to the north-western tribes in their appearance.

These people bury their dead underneath the hut which was lately inhabited by the deceased, after which the relatives go for a long canoe journey, staying away some months. This is done for sanitary reasons evidently, as the bodies are buried so near the surface that the smell would in all probability make any one sleeping in the hut sick, but they say it is because the spirit of the departed stays in his late residence for some time after his death, and eventually finding no one to torment goes away for good; the surviving relatives then return and remain there as formerly. No doubt, the coral acts in much the same manner as quicklime, and disposes of the decomposing portions of the dead body in a short time.

Matukanaputa lies but a few miles from Byning Bay, which is a considerable indentation in the coast, having deep water almost entirely throughout, but there is an anchorage for small vessels between a reef and the eastern side of the bay. Our first anchorage here was close in shore, on the western side near the head of the bay, and it was in this place that many of the Byning bushmen came down to see us. They were very timid at first, but by much persuasion we succeeded in getting one man who was bolder than the rest to swim off, and coming alongside I gave him some red cloth and some beads, at the same time showing him a yam, and saying, " Yau gulia op " ("I will pay for yams"). He was evidently very much frightened, but finding no harm was done him they eventually became more venturesome, and many came off bringing yams. On examining the bay in a boat I found that there was an anchorage between the reef on the eastern side and the mainland, that there was also a small temporary village on shore at this spot. I therefore moved the vessel round, and the next day there was quite a crowd of natives occupying the village, which before had been almost deserted. As women and children were amongst them, I had no hesitation in landing, and I was treated in consequence to a quite (to me) novel dance, though such are evidently the fashion among these bushmen. The women and men both took part in it, and were dressed in highly ornamental and coloured chasubles (I can call them nothing else) made of tapa, and coming down to a peak at the waist before and behind, covering the breast, stomach, and back, having holes for the head and arms; in some cases only half a one was worn, either before or behind, tied round the neck and arms with a string. Some of these men wore a waist wrapper, also highly ornamental and stained different colours; in both cases the predominating colours being black, red, and white, whilst in some few yellow was used; they danced in much the same fashion as the Eastern New Britain natives, with bunches of grass and ferns in their hands, and their heads bound round with circles of coloured grass.

The whole of the shore of this bay is thickly covered with bushes and trees, as indeed is the whole coast-line from it to Open Bay; and appears to be a belt of dense vegetation, which extends inland a greater or less distance according to the lay of the mountains, but as soon as the ground begins to rise, the land becomes more open, and grassy plains take the place of thick bush.

I am of opinion that the coast from this bay to Cape Gloucester, the western extremity of the island, has never been visited by white men before. The manner of the natives, the great discrepancies of the existing charts, and scarcity of places named by Europeans, are my reasons for coming to this conclusion. Those places that are so named have evidently to my mind been seen in passing and at a considerable distance off, by the extreme vagueness with which they are delineated on the charts. Thus, in leaving Byning Bay we felt that we were entering upon a new world. No doubt, had D'Entrecasteaux lived, more would have been known of this very important island; the little that is known of this northern part is due to him, indeed it was the scene of his last labours.

On leaving Byning Bay the navigation along the

coast becomes intricate and dangerous in the highest
degree ; reefs and small covered patches are innumerable, whilst in the offing may be seen the breakers
heavily dashing on the barrier or outside reefs ; the
curious effect of this tropical atmosphere making the
stones and breakers appear in mirage high up in the
burning, cloudless sky.   Strange sights may be seen

RIVER SCENE IN NEW BRITAIN (BYNING).

as the sun rises and before the monsoon has come
up—perhaps a canoe being vigorously paddled upside
down some degrees above the horizon, trees also
grow up out of the ocean, and a fishing " woop " or
mark showing a fish-trap will appear, though miles
away, like a ship in full sail.

I am only sorry that I was not enabled to make
a more accurate acquaintance with the natives on

this coast, as time would not allow of it. I therefore had to content myself with making a survey of the coast, and gaining what information I could from the natives that I fell in with, rather than by travelling much on shore; indeed I do not know that this would have been possible, or that the natives themselves would have allowed it, as those that we did meet (other than the Matukanaputa men) were very timid and difficult to hold intercourse with even in their canoes, except perhaps those at E'Watto.

Cape Lambert is spoken of by the natives, I believe, for it is difficult always to determine the precise spot of which they speak, as Mutucorrangi; it is a bold and rocky headland covered to the top of its cliffs with vegetation. About twelve miles to the north-west of it lie a chain of reefs running in a southerly direction, Wreck Reef being the most northerly one we examined (it was called so from our meeting with a sad accident there, of which more hereafter); but the natives tell me the reefs extend round outside the Scilly Islands and join those to the eastward of Matukanaputa. The Scilly Isles are small and rocky; there are six in all, but are uninhabited, serving only as a place of call for the Matukanaputa men in their raids on Byning or in their turtle fishing. A little further on is a point called Corroka; here there is a small village of fishing huts used by Matukanaputa natives; there is also a fine river, but the bar is very shallow, and though there is no surf, it would prevent a boat of any size entering. However, we pulled our small dingy over, and ascended about three miles, until stopped by driftwood and shallows.

The scenery was perfect, tropical verdure of the most luxurious growth thrusting itself into the water —dracœnas, crotans, and hibiscus, and ferns mixed in the wildest profusion; overhead were stately palms waving in the breeze that we could not feel, whilst far ahead in the distance are to be seen the glorious mountains of Byning towering in rugged grandeur.

There are large quantities of fresh-water fish in these rivers, and as they will take a fly I have had some good sport, from either the shore or the boat, with this kind of bait, using for a rod a long supple piece of bamboo. Some of the fish resemble in shape our pike, but the stripes on the back are yellow. The largest, however, and those I caught most of, were a kind of carp, with large black spots on their tails and fins; there were numerous other species, but as I had no spirits to put them into I refrained from catching more than would suffice for a meal. Crocodiles swarm in these rivers, large, middle size, and quite little fellows; the latter are excellent food, tasting much like chicken. The eggs I do not care for, they are too strong and fishy, but the natives delight in them. At every turn in the river we saw a colony of crocodiles of all sizes flop off the bank into the water, where they had been previously lying catching flies. They do it in this manner: they take up a position on the bank, and remain perfectly motionless with their mouths open; flies, attracted by the peculiar musky smell of the saliva in their mouths, settle by swarms inside the open jaws; presently there is a sharp snap, and a hundred or so of flies are entombed. I was not aware before I saw this that crocodiles were fly-catchers as well as fish, flesh and fowl eaters.

We saw no traces of any natives except those few huts at the mouth of the river, but the further we went the more open the country grew, and the more rocky grew the bed of the river. We had Rover with us in the boat, and we soon determined never to take him with us again on a river expedition, as the crocodiles seemed to think he had been brought for their special delectation, for they came up round the boat, and would only leave when splashed at with an oar; indeed, one fellow took hold of one of the blades in his mouth and left the mark of his teeth in it. Rover seemed particularly enraged at their want of courtesy in staring so, and barked furiously at them, which only made them worse. I was anxious not to fire at them for fear of frightening away any of the natives that might be camped on the river bank, though we saw none. However, we got back to the vessel without any accident and enjoyed our fish much.

Leaving Corroka, the next point arrived at is called Sulla; there a grand view is obtained of Mount Fitzgerald, named after a gentleman in Sydney who was most kind in assisting me in this expedition. It is the highest peak in the Byning range, and cannot be much less than five thousand feet in height, though I was unable to obtain its altitude. It is rocky and rugged, as are all these mountains, looking as though piled together by a race of giants. We constantly met canoes from Matukanaputa either returning with turtle or starting for "Sem-si-gorro," their chief station on this coast. They were always willing to show us a good place for anchorage, and we got much fish and black-edged pearl-shell from them, as well as quantities of the small shells, of which the New Britain and Duke of York money is made, and which is found in large quantities on the sand-flats in shallow water here. These they take to Matukanaputa, and from this place it gradually passes to the eastern tribes, where I was told by the natives that they did not know whence it came, though undoubtedly many of the chiefs did.

To the eastern tribes this coast is known by the general name of Nukani, which I fancy is the name given to any place that they know nothing about. Sollass-solla is the next point; here the reefs and sandbanks are innumerable; indeed, it would be impossible to have positioned them all with my small staff of two men; however, I took cross bearings of the principal in spite of being often up to our waists in water and occasionally having to drive off a shark or two who would flop on to the reefs, churning the water with their tails like a small steamer in ballast. The natives were very much frightened at the compass and other instruments, which was perhaps a good thing, as they kept a respectful distance in their canoes whilst operations were going on.

The next place of importance is Sem-si-gorro. This is the chief temporary fishing station of the Matukanaputa natives. It is on a small island that they have their huts built, where they are perched on every available spot. The island itself is about seventy or eighty feet high, rocky and covered with vegetation, having a sand-spit running from it towards the mainland. This being partly covered with water at high tide, in it are sunk a great number of forked stakes on which the canoes rest when not in use, to keep them out of the water in order that they may not be worm-eaten, as they assuredly would if left stationary in it too long. The mainland is here covered with mangrove swamps and salt-water creeks, running inland a considerable distance, which swarm with crocodiles. It was at this place that I obtained three of these reptiles, with the intention of trying how they might be tamed; two were quite young, and the third was about four-and-a-half feet long. The younger ones I found it hard to feed, as they seemed to care for nothing but fresh fish, but the larger one would eat anything, and the cook used to swear that Croaker, as he was called, ate his napkins, but I never saw him do it, though I have seen him put away a piece of sole-leather. The two younger ones died, but Croaker lived and became so tame he would come when called. I had also two fine snakes (pythons) that were excessively tame—one was twelve feet long, the other a little under nine feet. In fact, what with crocodiles, snakes, cuscus, wallaby, a native pig, dogs, and a cat, with at one time a cassowary, I used to say we could start a menagerie when we arrived in Australia; then we had a parrot as well that used to talk New Britain language, but by degrees picked up English, and would call the dogs so plainly that they were quite taken in and appeared awfully disgusted when they found it out; but he took to laughing one day, and I think he laughed for two hours without stopping and then fell down dead.

In the event of its being too rough for these native fishermen to go fishing, they remain on the island either mending their nets or making fresh turtle lassoes. The former are made and mended with a bobbin very like ours fashioned out of bamboo; the nets are composed of fine twine, knotted in the same way as ours, which consists of the fibre obtained from a creeping vine or from the bark of a tree. The turtle ropes are much rougher and made from strips of bark twisted together, and are about ten to twelve fathoms long, with a slip noose at one end; this is thrown from the canoe over the head of the turtle, or sometimes a man swims with it over his arm, and seizing the turtle by one of the front fins slips it over the head and fin, at the same time pulling it tight, taking the other end to his canoe, where the turtle is hauled in. They are very expert at this method, and will often catch as many as six large turtle in one day; they also go on the sandbanks at night in the laying season, and turn the turtle as they come up to lay their eggs. A man will sometimes float with a log under his stomach until he approaches close enough to the turtle to spear it with a javelin which is fastened to the end of this turtle rope ; but this is never done unless the turtle is to be eaten at once, as when dead it soon becomes unfit for food.

Should these natives be without fire they obtain it by rubbing a sharpened piece of hard stick against the inside of a piece of dried split bamboo. This has a natural dust clinging to it on the inside that ignites as soon as the necessary friction has been given and smoulders until some dried grass be added, when it is blown into a flame, by which means a fire is soon started. They sometimes use a soft piece of wood when bamboo is not easily procured, but it takes longer to ignite.

When fishing is ended and each canoe is loaded with turtle, the natives desert Sem-si-gorro and return to Matukanaputa. There are certain times when a man of this tribe may not go fishing, when one of his women is *enciente* or during the full of the moon ; in either case the spirits of departed ancestors are particularly vicious, and if one hears of a canoe being capsized and a man drowned (which does occasionally happen, though very seldom) that man must have been fishing at full moon. In the former case the man must stop at home to prevent the spirits taking away the life of the expected baby, by sucking its breath from it ; if the child dies in spite of all his precautions, they say he did not fight for it enough with the spirits. When in want of women for their young men to marry (as they may not marry into their own tribe) they make a raid against the bush tribes of Byning, and seize the young women, eating the bodies of the men killed or taken prisoners. The women soon become reconciled to their new homes, as they will take part in similar feasts on subsequent occasions.

As these natives appear to know the names of all the different places on the coast beyond Sem-si-gorro, I presume they travel along it as far as Willaumez Island, though we did not meet any more Matukanaputa canoes after leaving it.

CHAPTER IX.

THE next point is called Pondo, a tongue of land
running some little distance out from the main, on
the southern side of which is a cozy little anchorage
for a small vessel. On approaching this point a
remarkable red patch may be observed high up on
the side of one of the mountains, looking very like a
landslip. I should say it was probably very red
sandstone or red ochre, which seems to abound on
this coast. From this point may also be seen loom-
ing in the distance Torcoro, Unamungo, and Pucani-
cambula, the three huge volcanoes called on the chart
the Father and Sons; indeed they may occasionally
be seen after rounding Sulla Point in clear weather.

One can quite appreciate the feeling that the old
explorers must have had when suddenly sighting

some unknown land in an unknown sea, the imagination strung to the uttermost, not knowing what the next turn of the coast-line may bring them upon. Even to us who know that the supernatural is impossible, it is full of intense and almost breathless suspense and anticipation.

We next passed a small headland called Forrin, after passing which may be seen a waterfall at the head of the Unamula or Holmes River. Seeing such a waterfall high up on a mountain, where it appears to fall over a cliff that drops sheer into the valley below, led me to suppose that there must be a river of considerable size running into the sea on this coast not far off; indeed the natives at Sem-si-gorro told me that such was the case, though I had my doubts of it, from the closeness of the mountains to the coast, for I supposed there was not room for a large river to accumulate, and thought they must have somewhat exaggerated the size. However, a few miles further on we came to the mouth of a large river, which, judging by the shoaling of the water some miles from the coast, must carry with it from inland large deposits of mud. I sailed as close as I dared to go in the vessel, and then launched the boat. After crossing the bar, which I fear would prevent a vessel of any size from entering, being about one-and-a-half fathoms in the deepest part, we entered the river, which is a grand one, gradually widening from the mouth to about three-quarters of a mile.

Seeing no sign of natives we went on; the scene

WATERFALL OF HOLMES RIVER, OPEN BAY.   *To face page* 211.

was grand and beautiful to the highest degree, tropical vegetation in its wildest luxuriance covered the banks, palms and ferns dipping their graceful fronds in the water, whilst from other trees hung creepers with flowers of the brightest hues; the smaller shrubs seemed to have gone wild with colour. Birds of all descriptions and shade darted in and out amongst the trees; the white and blue kingfisher, the little brilliant sun-bird, parrots of all colours screamed at us from above, whilst further off we could hear the shrill note of the magapode, and above all would come the hoarse cry and the rushing sound of the hornbill; flocks of pigeons wheeling round a feeding tree, and cooing to each other, added a softer note to swell the wonderful harmony. We went straight on, fresh beauty meeting our eyes at each turn; I felt as though I could not speak, but only drink in the glorious sight with my eyes.

We met with no signs of any natives and advanced about four miles, passing the mouths of several other good-sized streams pouring their water into the main river. Soon it began to get narrower and eventually shallower. We continued advancing by hauling the boat over the shallows and driftwood which would impede our progress every now and then. Presently we could distinguish that the roaring we had heard for some time was the waterfall; in about half-an-hour we came in sight of it. I cannot attempt to describe it, the illustration may help to give the reader some little idea of it, but the top seemed lost in mist, and indeed it would be impossible to say how far it dropped, but I should think a clear four hundred feet without seeming to touch or be broken in its descent by anything; it falls into a large pool, which has evidently been worn away by the continued drop of the water and is of considerable size. We did not go up to this pool in the boat, but I landed and walked round to a spot whence I could get a good view of the falls; it is evidently the head of the main river, although there is another stream running round the foot of the mountain into the pool, but its body of water is small compared with that of the waterfall. I should say that the fall was about twenty yards across as far up as I could see and spreads a good deal at the bottom, but it is so fringed with bushes and shrubs that it is difficult to judge what the real width might be. How I longed for a camera to take a photograph of it. It was with reluctance that I left this beautiful sight and returned to the boat, when it took us but a comparatively short time to return to the vessel, the stream carrying us down without need of much assistance from the oars.

After rounding Sandy Point or Nologun we found ourselves in deep water again, and entering Open Bay we still continued to hug the coast, as indeed we were obliged to by reason of the reefs surrounding Turtle Island. Shortly afterwards we came to the entrance of a beautiful little land-locked harbour, for which I believe the native name to be " Nemisocco," and which we named Port Powell. It has an entrance about a quarter-of-a-mile wide, but extends on the inside to the width of one mile by one and three-quarters in depth, having an even muddy bottom of fifteen fathoms. The harbour is well sheltered, the banks are thickly wooded, and fresh water may be obtained at a short distance from the eastern shore.

This port when we visited it was literally swarming with turtles, green, loggerhead, and hawksbill of all sizes, several of which we caught without much difficulty. At the north end of the harbour is a salt-water creek running into it, which was full of fish as well as young crocodiles. This port would make a capital place for a vessel to lay up to refit in, there being plenty of wood to be obtained on the surrounding shores.

Turtle Island is evidently a spot that is visited by the natives in their search for turtle, and judging by the large number of turtle bones lying about on it, they must find it a profitable hunting ground.

From this place we could obtain a fine view of the Father and Sons volcanoes, which tower up in their solitary grandeur about eighteen or twenty miles distant. We could see at intervals clouds of smoke bursting up from the summit of the stately Father as though some huge pulse were at work deep down in the bowels of the earth; the volume, however, was always greater at sunrise and sunset than at any other time. The North Son from where we were appeared to be an island, which I have little doubt was the cause of the Le Danseur Island on the Admiralty charts. There is a small island close under the North Son — so small is it, in fact, that it would easily escape notice if passed at any distance off.

On leaving Port Powell we passed a spot termed Ullamorn, which lies a little further to the southward.

At the head of Open Bay there is a slight bend in the coast-line towards the east; the land is flat and uninteresting, but mountains can be seen at some distance inland. Further on comes a river called Ulla, which I fancy must be the native name here for a stream of fresh water.

E'Watto was the first place after leaving Semsi-gorro that we found natives, and they appeared distinctly to remember having seen my vessel before, in company with one that they expressed as "puffing

and shrieking." Their imitation was so graphic that
I at once concluded that they meant the *Duke of York*
mission steam-launch which had accompanied me to
Spacious Bay, and which lies immediately on the other
side of the island. This bay I afterwards found to
be separated from Open Bay only by a narrow
isthmus of four or five miles in breadth, the isthmus
for the greater part being plain land, but inter-

MAN NATIVE, E'WATTO, OPEN BAY, NEW BRITAIN.

spersed here and there with volcanic upheavals.
These natives were very friendly towards us, and
brought us off some fresh water to fill our water-
casks, also yams. We bought a variety of ornaments and implements from them. I found them to
be identical with those that I had bought in Spacious
Bay. These natives have a very strong resemblance
to those of the north-east coast of New Guinea.

Their language is totally different from that of the natives of the north and east coasts of Gazelle Peninsula; they do not appear to be afflicted to the same extent with that disagreeable disease buckwar, and are also of a much lighter shade of brown; their houses are far superior, though they have somewhat the same beehive shape, but are higher. Their canoes, although ornamented with great taste and profusion, are, I am forced to admit, very inferior to those of the more northern tribes, but perhaps they have less occasion for them. They are evidently a shore-going tribe, and described to me by signs how the sun came up in the morning when they started to go across the isthmus, and it was about half-way down the other side before they got to Spacious Bay, which they described by stretching their hands out over Open Bay, and then touching my vessel, making a puffing and whistling noise, then pointing across the land in the Spacious Bay direction. I find natives are exceedingly clever at signs, and I have never had the least difficulty in making them understand or in understanding them myself.

The coast after leaving E'Watto is broken up by many embayments, but as they are very deep are little use as harbours. At Corlaili we found more natives, and again at Matīyu, which is just within Hixson Bay, which I called after that courteous and kind-hearted gentleman who is the President of the Marine Board of New South Wales. They are all of the same type as those at E'Watto, and were civil and friendly. The whole of this part of the country seems to be a field of obsidian, huge blocks of it lying on the shores like lumps of glass; the natives apply it to all manner of uses, for shaving their heads, bleeding themselves, cutting and carving wood, and also for circumcision, which is a general habit amongst them here; they all wear a waist covering of fowlash highly ornamented and stained with different colours and patterns. At E'Watto, where I landed, I was surrounded by a crowd of women, who evidently were under the impression I was merely painted white, as they rubbed my hands and face with their fingers and then looked at them to see if any of the white had come off. One ugly old lady opened the front of my shirt in spite of opposition, and was evidently giving the others a lecture on the habits and customs of the white man. She then rubbed and pinched my flesh until it was red, on seeing which the others began to shout and yell with astonishment. However, one of the men came to my assistance, and drove them all off with a stick. I am sorry to say I did not visit their town as I was too ill with fever, and it required a considerable climb to get up to it; so I had to content myself with sitting on the beach and talking sign language to the men. They, however, kindly provided me with four cocoa-nuts to drink, for which I was very thankful; they appear a very intelligent race of people, although they are undoubtedly cannibals.

After leaving Hixson Bay, which is wrongly spelt

on the charts, and which we did not examine very
closely, we passed Heath Island (the small island
I mentioned before as lying close under the foot
of the North Son), which has a very narrow
passage with huge cliffs on each side, between it and
the mainland, but bearing no comparison with the
Lé Danseur Island of the old charts. We then came
to Cape Deschamp or Torcoro, though I do not feel
at all sure that this name applies to the point, or
only the mountain of the North Son; indeed I do
not feel certain about either of the native names
of the points that are immediately beneath these
three mountains.

The Father is the highest of the three, and stands
between his two Sons; the sketch will give a slight
idea of them. The Father and South Són are active
volcanoes, the Father being the most active of the
two; it throws up great volumes of smoke and a
substance which viewed from the foot of the volcano
looks like mud, though it may be ashes. The present
crater has so evidently grown up out of the ruins of
an older one, that I am inclined to think it must be
formed of something more than merely volcanic ashes,
though I do not think it can be lava. The South
Son does not eject such a volume of smoke, neither is
there apparently any solid substance thrown up
with it, though there is the same appearance as of an
old and new crater. Both these volcanoes are well
wooded up to the old craters, but the slopes of the
new ones are quite destitute of any vegetation.
The Father is about four thousand feet high, and the

South Son about three thousand feet; the North Son is much lower than either of the others, being only one thousand three hundred feet, and to all appearance is an extinct volcano; its crater, however, has the look of having been very much shattered at some former time by a severe eruption. Here some natives brought off great lumps of grey obsidian. Long Point is a long low point of land immediately below the Father Mountain. Low Point is a similar point immediately below the South Son.

Duportail Island lies four-and-a-half miles due west from Long Point. It has two mountains, one a conical peak and the other

THE FATHER AND SONS, FROM DUPORTAIL ISLAND.

a volcano with a very peculiar crater, much resembling the mouth of a huge whale, as if indeed the mountain had fallen in half at the summit. It does not emit much smoke, except after rain, when there is a much larger volume; it is well clothed with vegetation on all sides of the crater, but is quite bare between the two summits. The whole

HEAD-DRESS, NATIVE MAN, DUPORTAIL ISLAND, NEW BRITAIN.

island is thickly wooded and seemingly contains a large population.

Many canoes started off for us, from the occupants of which we obtained several ornaments; they were very timid about coming alongside, but came from the shore with the evident intention of trading; but when they approached us I suppose their hearts

DECEPTION POINT.

See page 222.

DUCKTAIL ISLAND, FROM EXPECTATION STRAITS.

To face page 221.

failed them, and it was with difficulty we persuaded them to come alongside. They are the same aquiline-featured people as those of Open Bay, but they wore a head-dress that I had not seen before, though it was frequent with the natives further to the west-ward. This consisted of a number of rings made of plaited cane and edged with the small shell that is used in the North Peninsula as money, and are worn pressed down tight above the ears, each ring being smaller in width as they rise to the top of the head. These are placed on the head of a man-child when quite an infant, and are not removed until they are fifteen or sixteen years of age, when they are cut off and others of a larger size put on. The consequence of this is that the men's heads are compressed just above the ears, though the mark is hidden by the rings that they wear. I was successful after a great deal of gesticulation in obtaining a set from a youth who evidently had not long had his second set put on, for they came off comparatively easily; their hair stands up above the rings in quite a tuft. I am under the impression that they are worn to protect their heads from the blow of a club, and that thus wearing them early makes a ridge in the skull that prevents their being struck or falling off.

There are two small islands to the south-west with a particularly dangerous sunken reef lying between them and Duportail Island; indeed we were nearly on the top of it, as in smooth weather it does not break, and appears to be covered with some kind of green sea-weed that prevented us seeing it until quite close to it.

From Low Point to Hummock Head or Quass the land is one vast tract of volcanic upheavals, that are now apparently quiescent, but cannot have been long so, as the country is covered with small craters and rents. Their being covered with vegetation is, I think, no argument against their having been in action within recent years, as in this rich soil and tropical climate a forest will spring up in a short time where before was a barren waste of pumice.

Beyond Quass the land becomes low and flat and uninteresting, indeed the only high land on the coast at all is Chard, Vessy and MacDonald Islands, named after three gentlemen who kindly interested themselves in this expedition. Commodore Bay appeared to be full of shoals, with Norton Island in the centre, but we did not enter the bay as it looked very uninviting, the banks on the south side and west end being covered with mangrove swamps; so we contented ourselves with observing that the high land to the north was not an island but a peninsula of no ordinary kind, having the most extraordinary collection of mountains I have ever seen in so small a space. It is not surprising that observers at a distance should suppose it to be an island, as all the land at the back is so low that it could not be seen more than about ten miles off, and I feel convinced that few if any European ships have been as close as that to this strange peninsula. The sketch will give the reader a better idea of it than a long description, yet I cannot help mentioning Mount Pyramid, which name it bears on account of its very remarkable shape; in fact it is difficult to imagine that so perfect a pyramid could have been formed without human agency. All the mountains on this peninsula are of volcanic formation, being mostly entire volcanoes.

When off Jenkins Island (named after another kind supporter of this expedition) we observed a number of canoes that started from Island Point and came over to the island, which I do not think is inhabited, but merely a fishing station, as we could not see any houses on it. They had evidently seen us, and had come out to look at the strange monster as our vessel must have appeared to them. We stood in for Jenkins Island in order to try and persuade them to trade with us, but as soon as they saw us approaching they all left their canoes and bolted on shore into the bush. I waved a green bough and beckoned them to come to us, but it was of no use, they were too much frightened, and hid themselves amongst the scrub. Therefore, as there was no convenient place for anchorage, I had to stand off again, and as soon as the natives saw this they came back to their canoes, but although I shortened sail and used every endeavour to get them to come up to us, they kept about a mile off. At last I got some half cocoa-nut husks, and filling them with some beads and red cloth set them adrift over the stern. When the canoes came up with them I could see with my glasses how astonished and excited the natives

were.   After some little time, which was given up to
examining the marvels they had just picked up, one
canoe advanced in front of the others, and a man
stood up in the bow and threw a cocoa-nut as far as
he could towards us.   On seeing this evident act of
friendship I bouted ship and stood back for the
cocoa-nut, but as soon as they saw us coming for
them away they went as fast as they could paddle.
This was very provoking; however, we picked up
the cocoa-nut, and as I had no wish to stay all night
amongst the numerous reefs that surround this shore
we had to stand out for open water and towards Fitz
Island.

I am not at all surprised at the natives behaving
in the way that they did, for it must be indeed a
marvellous sight to them; in fact if we could only
put ourselves in their place on such an occasion I do
not much think we should have the courage to go
after so strange an apparition at all.

It was a very lucky thing for us that I did not
remain any longer in the vicinity of the reefs, as
about eight o'clock P.M. a fearful thunderstorm came
up, the worst I have ever seen, with wind and rain;
the lightning seemed to be all round us, and the
thunder was deafening.   Whilst it was raging we
felt the vessel apparently strike heavily, and then roll
from side to side with much violence.   We soon had
the lead over, but found no bottom at fifty fathoms.
It then occurred to me that it was the shock of an
earthquake we had felt.   Two more followed, but
neither of them so severe as the first.   I cannot

describe the sensation better than by saying it was just as if we had struck on a coral reef and then slid off the other side; the vessel seemed to shake from stem to stern and rolled a good deal.

Next morning we stood over towards Cape Campbell: this is the north point of Willaumez Island, and is a high precipitous foreland. It is called its present name after a gentleman in the Mines Department of New South Wales, who took an active interest in the expedition. Du Faur Island is also named after the chief instigator of this I hope not altogether useless expedition: he is indeed one who seldom allows a chance to escape him of assisting geographical research.

On the western side of Willaumez Island we saw several canoes coming out from the shore to have a look at us, but they would not venture closer than some three or four hundred yards or so. I was determined to get these fellows alongside if it was possible, so after waving my green branch (kept for the special purpose) I wrapped a piece of red cloth round a piece of wood and threw it towards them. For some time they hesitated, but at last one canoe ventured a little towards it, and then stopped again; but a young fine-looking fellow at length standing up threw down his paddle as if to say (perhaps he did actually say it), " Here goes, I'll chance it," and jumped from the canoe and began swimming towards the red cloth, which he soon got hold of and returned to the canoe. I immediately threw another piece of wood with a string of beads, taking

care that it should fall closer to the vessel than the
first; the same young man again ventured and
secured the prize. Their excitement had been great
on the return of the red cloth, but it was nothing to
that on the arrival of the beads: they shouted and
halloed, and no doubt would have danced had they
not been in a canoe. Each man tried it by putting
it round his neck and round his arm to see how it
would look as a necklace and armlet; they then
returned to the other canoes to show them. In the
meantime I got a piece of red cloth and waved it
over the side to show them I had lots more if they
would come and get it. However, I found that this
was useless, so had to resort to the old plan of
throwing sticks with red cloth or beads on it into
the water. This time two canoes started for the stick
and paddled slowly up to it, but on the bow of each
a man stood up with a spear in his hand all ready to
throw. As there was only one stick in the water I
threw another, only taking care it should drop even
closer to the ship; then the same young fellow
plunged overboard and got it; but seeing me hold
out some beads over the ship's side he ventured to
come up and take them, but was evidently half sinking
with fright. However, he soon found that no harm
was intended, and went off with his beads delighted,
as he deserved to be, for I think it was the pluckiest
thing I had seen done whilst in these islands.

Not to weary you with continued repetition I may
as well state that after a great deal more persuasion
we got them alongside, but in each canoe was a man

standing up with a spear all ready at a moment's notice to take the defensive. However, as we took no notice whatever of this, and finding that we had no intention otherwise than trading with them for ornaments, &c., they eventually laid them down and

NATIVE OF WILLAUMEZ ISLAND, NEW BRITAIN.

entered into the negotiations. If a sail flapped or one of the men moved at all quickly along the deck, they were up again in a moment; but I cannot say that they presented a very warlike appearance, for they were shaking all over with nervousness and fear. We bought a large collection

of necklaces, armlets, earrings, head-dresses, as well
as some spears, stone tomahawks, and clubs. The
spears were of the rudest description, as were the
tomahawks ; the clubs much resembled a policeman's
staff but longer ; the ornaments were good, and some
of the armlets beautifully made. Almost everything
was ornamented with that same little shell that is

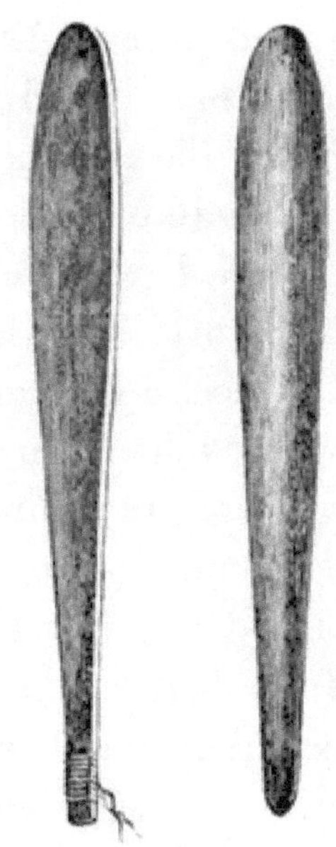

CLUBS, CAPE HOSKINS, NEW BRITAIN.

used so generally all over New Britain. They all
wore the same curious head-dress that I mentioned
before, and also had their loins covered with fowbash, slightly ornamented, but not so highly as those
of the men of E'Watto. They are the same race
as the Open Bay men, having the same clearly cut
features. Of course we saw none of the women.

The lobes of their ears are not so extended as those of the natives of Gazelle Peninsula, and they are altogether a finer race of people than the former.

The Islands of Du Faur, Giequel, Raoul, and Willaumez are all volcanic, nearly all the mountains having the appearance of being craters, although we did not observe that any were in active eruption.

On leaving these islands the land appeared to be low and uninviting, and to have little appearance of any volcanoes, except one island that we did not examine, and which in the distance appeared to be all peaks and points, like a collection of huge termites' nests. Indeed I was really too ill with fever to do any more work, and the two other men were almost as bad. Aleck I had left behind with his own people, and my cook had run away in Duke of York, so that there were only three of us all told, still that was quite enough to work the little vessel had we been all able bodied, but this I am sorry to say we were far from being. No sooner was one able to crawl on deck than another would be struck down with that terrible malady, which once having got hold is not easily shaken off, and our provision was getting scanty; I therefore determined to run on to Cape Gloucester, where I hoped to be able to get some pigs, or at all events some yams or taro.

We passed French Islands on our way, where we endeavoured to get the natives off to us, but they were too timid, therefore kept on our course for Cape Gloucester. As we approached it we saw a great volume of smoke hanging over the land which obscured the tops of the mountains, and on approaching closer found that it was caused by innumerable volcanoes, small and large, all in violent eruption. It was a most extraordinary sight; there must have been some hundred or more all belching fire and smoke, indeed the land seemed all on fire. We anchored some distance off the shore at the end of a reef, so as to be well away from the natives for the night.

When night came on the sight was wonderful. Flames seemed to cover the mountainous point of land, and it would have been easy to read a book by the light; the air was full of fine ashes covering and making everything a light grey colour; indeed it was difficult to breathe comfortably. Tupinier Island was in eruption also, and the noise made by them all was like low continuous thunders.

In the morning we moved in closer to the shore, but saw no signs of natives. This was very disappointing, and I decided to try Rook Island. We therefore left this burning bay and tried to cross Dampier Straits, but found it was blowing a heavy gale of wind from the south-east, with the sea running high. We beat backwards and forwards trying to make Rook Island, but there was so strong a current running through Dampier Straits, that we could not make any way against it. We tried for two days without success, and had to keep constantly at the pumps, as the topsides of the vessel had become so dry that in the heavy sea we experienced they leaked badly. At last a big sea struck the rudder and swept it away like a rotten stick. There was now no chance of reaching Rook Island; so nearly worn out, with the rudder gone and vessel leaking, there was nothing for it but to run back; and after fixing a temporary rudder with some oars, &c., we ran back to a small bay about twenty miles to the eastward of Cape Gloucester.

After some little search we found a suitable sandbank about thirty yards from the beach on which to ground the vessel, in order to fix a rudder sufficiently durable to take us back to Duke of York, where we might obtain wood to make a new one. The rise and fall of the tide being about four feet, we laid an anchor out ahead on the sandbank which was nearly covered at high water. By this means we hove the vessel to a spot where she would lay high and dry on the fall of the tide.

As we were waiting this result, a canoe came round a point not far away, making straight for us. When they were at a short distance off they stopped, and an old man held up two or three small yams, evidently offering them for sale. I at once intimated that I would buy them, and he came alongside and I gave him some beads for them. He showed me the remains of an old crucifix, which he carried hung round his neck, and which I tried to purchase from him, but he would not part with it. I made signs to him as to where it came from; he put his hands together as if at prayer and said "lotu." This is the common word used by all missionaries everywhere, I believe, to signify religion. He then pointed towards Rook Island, at which place I afterwards found out there had been a Roman Catholic mission-station, the members of which had either been killed or died—I do not know which, but at all events it had been abandoned some years.

The old native examined the vessel very carefully as well as the anchor that was on the sandbank, and then left us, evidently promising to return with more yams. Soon after the vessel took the ground, and we began to place the temporary rudder, but I found I could not work, as being so weak with fever I could hardly stand upright; so the other two went to work at it, and I had to retire below. I had not been below long when H—— shouted down the companion that there were a crowd of natives coming along the beach armed with spears, &c., and that their intentions did not seem very pacific.

I must say I felt more inclined to let them come just then than able to offer them any resistance if they meant hostility, but it would hardly do to lay down and die, no matter how bad I might feel; so I got up on deck, and we soon had the muskets loaded, some with rock salt, and the little swivels sponged and loaded, and were determined to show a stout resistance if necessary. I noticed that there were a large number of men on the beach some distance off, as well as several canoes full of men lying off the shore. All the party were armed with slings, spears, and stone tomahawks.

It presently occurred to me that Rover was on shore, and that this would be a good method of finding out their intentions, so we called him ; soon he came bounding out of the bush, whereupon several young men ran forward and threw their spears at him, however without hitting him ; he was soon on board. I then waved my green branch, but it was received with a shout of derision. I could now see that they meant mischief, so we waited quietly for them to make the first move ; and as we were unable to get off the sandbank until high water, all we could do was to defend ourselves as well as possible. They soon began the attack with a shower of stones from their slings, at the same time coming steadily along the beach towards us ; the stones rattled nastily enough amongst the rigging and against the ship's side. I now fired a bullet over their heads ; this was again received with a shout of derision, and they only came faster towards us, the canoes going out to the seaward side of us. I began to feel somewhat anxious as to whether these men were afraid of firearms or no, or whether their indifference arose from mere ignorance of their deadly nature.

They were now near enough to use their spears, and began throwing them with considerable precision. However, we reserved our fire until they were near enough to feel the effects of the salt with which I proposed to dose them first. Some of them, about twenty, soon crossed the short channel of water that lay between the sandbanks and the shore and advanced with great confidence towards the bows of the vessel. In the meantime we had sat down under the bulwarks in order to be out of the way of the stones, and therefore not seeing us making any signs of defence they were led to imagine that they would have an easy victory. However, when they came close enough H—— and I both jumped up and fired together right into the midst of them. I never saw anything so ludicrous as the scene that followed. As we had taken the precaution to fire low the salt took effect on their bodies; they seemed actually too frightened to run away or feel the pain of the salt; however, they soon found their legs and ran for their lives. As they went we gave them another dose behind to make it even; but by the time they had got to the beach the salt began to take effect, and by their antics as they ran off I should say that they had had a lesson that they will be careful about having repeated.

The other natives, as soon as they saw their comrades run away, disappeared into the bush like magic, and the canoes also seemed anxious to get out of sight: amongst the former I had recognised our old friend of the yams and the crucifix. He had evidently learned one thing from the missionaries, and that was that white men's vessels are good plunder; but we have also perhaps taught them that it is not so easy to do it as they imagined. It certainly was a much more quickly gained victory than I had hoped for, and also without any bloodshed. We soon after got the temporary rudder finished, and getting our anchor up we hauled off into deep water and made sail on our return voyage to Duke

of York, but we were, alas, destined never to reach
that island in our brave little vessel.

We stood straight for Cape Lambert, and reached
it at the end of the second day. Wanting to anchor
I steered for a little bay just to the southward of it,
not wishing to be knocking about amongst the
innumerable shoals on the other side of the cape
at night-time with the vessel in a crippled state; but,
unfortunately, as we approached the land it fell calm,
and in spite of our sweeps the current carried us
away to the southward. As soon, however, as the
sun went down, but too late for us, a light breeze
sprang up, and all that we could do was to stand off
and on as near the shore as we dared to go in order
to keep clear of the reefs outside of us; there unfortunately was no moon that night.

We took the precaution to have a kedge anchor
hanging over the bows with ten fathoms of hawser
out; this was to bring us up if we got into shallow
water. We were all right up to two A.M., when a
heavy squall of wind and rain came drifting over
the land, quite obscuring it; and as we had to shorten
sail no doubt we drifted to the eastward much faster
than I was aware of. The squall was very heavy
whilst it lasted and soon put the sea up; it was also
quite impossible to see anything for the rain which
poured in torrents. About half-past two I noticed
a line of phosphorescent light in the water right
under our lea, which I knew meant that there was a
reef close to. I called to the others to put her about,
but she failed to answer the helm, and whilst making

a second trial a large sea caught the vessel and lifted her with a crash on to the reef that knocked us all off our feet. Here she lay hard and fast with the sea breaking over the stern as though it would dash her to pieces any minute, and which made her thump heavily on the rocks.

Towards daybreak the vessel began to leak, so we brought up everything we could out of the cabin and hold to the forecastle, and shortly after sunrise, the sea having much moderated, we placed the most valuable articles in the boat, when I and one of the men started off in it to a sandbank lying at some distance to the southward, which was the nearest place of safety to where the vessel was lying, intending to return for a fresh load and to bring off as many things as possible and place them there until we could make a raft to carry them to Materbert. However, on arriving at the sandbank to my surprise it was covered with Matukanaputa natives, who were there to catch turtle. As soon as they caught sight of our boat they all ran to seize their spears, clubs, and slings, apparently thinking that we were going to fight with them; so I went on shore with my hands up over my head, which is a sign of peaceable intentions, and told them my vessel was on shore and that I wanted to land my goods there, to which, after a considerable amount of talking, they agreed, but deeming it necessary that some one should stay there and look after them I sent back the man for another load, which he brought towards evening, and then returned again, as having but one boat it was wiser to leave it by the vessel in case she should break up during the night.

Thus left on the sandbank with fifty or sixty natives, who were in anything but a friendly mood, my first act was to see that my rifle and revolver were in a proper condition for defence ; next I pulled the boxes into a sort of protection for my back, and then sat down to watch through the night, lest they should steal anything. I could see by their talking together in groups and their side glances at me that they wanted very much to get hold of the boxes which we had landed. At last some of them came towards where I was sitting and began to sympathise with me, saying how sorry they were that my ship was ashore, and what a good man they considered me ; one villain even went so far as to shed tears. All the while they were speaking they were closing in around me. Too well used to natives to be taken in by this ruse, I stood up and told them in their own language to sit down and talk if they had anything to say ; for had I allowed them to get close up they would have rushed at me, knowing that I should not then have had room to use my musket or time to draw my revolver.

Being evidently taken by surprise, and perceiving that their design was detected, they sat down round me at a few yards' distance, and again commenced their protestations of friendship and sympathy ; but I fancied I heard one man say to another as they moved away, " We shall not eat white men to-night." This put me still more on the *qui vive*; so after listening to their protestations for some little while I told them that if they were really my friends they would go to Materbert and tell Tobrian (the chief I have mentioned before) that I wanted him to send me two or three of his largest canoes to take away my goods, and that if they would not do this (for which I offered to pay them handsomely), and came any closer to me, I should have to fire. At first they did not appear to like this idea at all, until one of them, an old man, succeeded in persuading them (as I afterwards discovered) to pretend to go away and see if I should fall asleep; they then went down to their canoes and paddled out into the darkness.

This did not satisfy me, for I know that these gentlemen seldom give up a project of this kind to which they have once made up their minds—besides, they could not be sure the boat would not return, when they would have had two instead of one to contend with, and this might account for their hesitation, for they will invariably use stratagem to gain an end rather than open force, if necessary. Indeed, when I think of the wretched state I was in through sickness I marvel that I was enabled to do what I did.

About one o'clock I fancied I heard a faint sound of paddles close by, and luckily having my glasses with me succeeded in making out three canoes creeping up very quietly, in each of which a man was standing up with a spear already poised trying to see if I were awake. I immediately shouted to them to go back if they did not wish me to fire, whereupon they quickly paddled away, and the rest of the canoes, which were only on the other side of the bank, followed suit and made off also. They did not trouble me again that night, and when morning broke there was no sign of them.

But a fresh cause for alarm now arose—the boat did not come off, and I began to fear that the two men on board the vessel had gone to sleep and been murdered, in which case there was no chance for me; for even if successful in keeping off the natives I had very little water and nothing to eat. Towards eleven o'clock a canoe appeared, and on nearing the sandbank a man stood up in it and hailed me, saying that he was a friend and wanted to speak to me. As he held his hands over his head to show that he had no arms I allowed him to land, when he commenced lamenting the wreck of the vessel, but I soon stopped his talking in that way, telling him it was all gammon, that the men from Matukanaputa had said the same thing the night before, and wanted to kill me afterwards by way of showing their sympathy, and asked him if he wished to do so also. "No," he said, " I have come to talk ; the Matukanaputa men are no good : it is a good thing you did not sleep last night or they would have killed and eaten you: do not go to sleep to-night : look out for your boat, they will kill the man in the boat, and then you have no water, and the man on board has little water, and you cannot go to him, and he cannot come to you, and they will catch

you when you sleep, and they say that there is plenty
of wood here to cook you, and that they do not know
how white men taste. I replied that he was my
friend for telling me all this, and that if he would go
to Tobrian and tell him I wanted some large canoes
to take away my things I would give him a big
present, but he said he could not do that as the
Byning men would kill him if they found it out; and
on my repeating the inducement he replied, "No,
no: the present is no good to a dead man;" so I had
to let him go away, after giving him a piece or two
of tobacco. Soon after this another canoe came up
manned by Matukanaputa men. One of them
hailed me for leave to come ashore and talk. Not
wishing to appear afraid of them I told him he
might come, which he did, accompanied by two or
three others, and carrying a coil of rope in his hand,
such as they generally use for catching turtle. I was
standing with my back to the boxes waiting for him
to come up, conjecturing at once what the rope was for.
" I have come," he said, " from Tobrian : is this canoe
large enough? come and look at it." Knowing
that he had not had time to go to Tobrian, and also
that he was a Matukanaputa man, I was on the look-
out for him. I asked him what he wanted with the
rope in his hand. He looked very much confused,
and said, "For turtle;" and I told him that turtle
were not caught in the day-time, and made him
give me the rope, adding that if I caught him
there again I would shoot him, and that he had
better go at once if he didn't wish me to do so

then. If I hadn't taken the rope from him, and he could have got me to move from the boxes, one of the other men would have rushed at me from behind, and he then would have fastened me round and round with the rope: they are very expert at catching turtle in this manner. Just as he was going off I caught sight of the boat returning; the man told me that they had had great difficulty in getting some of the cargo out of the hold, and that this had prevented his reaching the sandbank earlier. I sent back for the other man, thinking it best that we should all be together for the night.

Early in the morning both men started off well armed to the vessel again for another load. No sooner had they left the sandbank (it being yet dark) than I observed some fifteen or twenty canoes coming straight for it. Now the boat had brought the swivel gun the night before, so I quickly mounted it on a log and loaded it with a heavy charge and a handful of bullets, and then lay down quietly and waited for them to come up. Presently one of them came quite close, nearer and nearer, very cautiously. I clutched my firestick tightly, and laid the gun straight for him. "But hold on," I thought; "this fellow has come close to see if I am awake, and if I sham to be asleep he will go back and they will all come up, and give me a better chance of hitting some one." So I waited on quietly, and it turned out just as I had expected; the single canoe carefully reconnoitred, but as I was lying behind the stump of a tree they must have concluded that I was asleep, for they went back to the rest, and then all advanced together without making any noise. They had evidently watched for the boat to go away and then thought to catch me asleep. On they came, my fingers itched to apply the firestick to my gun ; "but, let them get a little closer," I thought. I could see a man in each canoe standing up to try and catch a sight of me. "A little closer, so that some of them can't escape." As they came I levelled. "A little closer," so, "now for them !" and down went the firestick—bang !—and then the most awful row I ever heard proceeded from the canoes, and they were off so quickly that I had no time to give them another dose. Whether any were killed or wounded I never discovered.

At daylight our boat returned, and the men brought me news that the natives had been on board the vessel and destroyed everything, breaking up even the compasses and side-lights, and throwing everything they did not want overboard, and had killed poor old Rover and taken his body away to eat.

That day we were left in peace, and we built a tent out of some of the sails that we had saved from the wreck ; but the following day, about eleven o'clock, we saw a large number of canoes coming from the mainland, and we accordingly prepared to give battle. They came on, however, without any hesitation until within about a hundred yards of the sandbank, when one canoe advanced without any arms, and one of the natives asked leave to come on shore, calling out at the same time that it was

Talong, a young sub-chief, whom I knew belonged to
Tobrian; so I allowed him to land, and he told me
that he had been sent by Tobrian to take myself and
my things to Materbert. I had some misgivings about
this message, as some of the men with him were
Matukanaputa men; but I knew that Talong was to
be relied upon, and, as our boat could not carry half
the things, thought it best to chance it; so I left the
rifles with the two men, and told them to come on in
the boat as soon as they could load it, and after
distributing the greater part of the goods in the
canoes, took my revolver and started off in Talong's
canoe. All went well until we got close in to the
mainland, when first one canoe made for the shore,
then another, and so on until they had nearly all
gone upon the beach. I turned round to Talong,
who was steering my canoe, and asked him, " Why
don't those men come on in their canoes?" He said
they were hungry, and that it was too hot; they
would go on again at night. "That's all gammon,"
I replied: "tell them to come on at once." He
went on shore to tell them this, and it was evident
that they were having a very excited discussion.
Presently he came back to the canoe and said, " They
want you to go on shore, and have something to eat,"
and then he added in a whisper, " Don't go; they will
kill you; let us go to Materbert quick, and get some
big canoes, and come and fight these men and get
back your things." Seeing that he was very much
excited, and trembling all over, and knowing there
was no time to be lost, I told him to jump in and

paddle as fast as he could for Cape Lambert. He was not long in complying with my injunctions, his men paddling as if for their lives. No sooner did the others see that we were escaping, than ten canoes started in pursuit, yelling like demons. On we went, Talong's men doing their utmost; but in spite of all their exertions it became evident in about half-an-hour that they were gaining upon us. Every now and then a man in one or other of the pursuing canoes would stand up, and then either a spear or a stone would come with a whir or splash close alongside us. However, I would not fire yet, although Talong kept urging me to do so, for the canoe was moving too much for me to get a steady aim, and I had not any ammunition to throw away. Nearer and nearer they came, and the stones from their slings were coming unpleasantly close. I raised the revolver, and resting it on my arm let fly at the leader. One man dropped his arm and paddle together, struck somewhere about the shoulder. When our fellows saw this they raised a great shout of triumph; but the others, not at all disconcerted, pushed on with even more vigour than before. The revolver went up again; this time they were considerably nearer, and I had just covered the steerer of the leading canoe, when Talong called out, "Mr. Powell, Mr. Powell, a big boat, look!" Just as I turned my head to look a stone passed within a few inches of me, and struck the man behind me in the back, knocking him over into the bottom of the canoe, where he lay apparently badly hurt. Most providential then was the appearance of the boat upon the scene. Our pursuers very soon caught sight of it also, and made off as fast as they had come.

We were not long in reaching our deliverer, which turned out to be one of Messrs. Godefroy's traders' boats from a long way to the eastward. It had come round Cape Lambert, the furthest point that a boat has ever been in that direction, this one never having been so far before, so that altogether it was a most fortunate escape. I soon explained matters to the white trader, and then we made sail and pulled after the retreating canoes; but on reaching the mainland found only empty boxes and canoes, the natives having taken away everything up into the bush with them, and as it would be useless to try and follow them without a strong party, we went off to look for my boat. This we shortly came up with, and then made sail for the traders' station. Thus I lost nearly everything of the anthropological collection made in this side of the island—I had but a few things left—the large assortment of land and sea conchology that I had been carefully getting together for Dr. Cox, of Sydney, my tame animals, in fact everything but my log sketches and field books, so that my survey work was saved. Luckily I had sent a large collection to Sydney, of clubs, spears, &c. However, I am thankful that my life was spared.

I was not long in getting round to Nodup, and from thence I crossed to Duke of York, where I found the *Renard* man-of-war schooner, Lieut. Commander Richards, who curiously happened to be an old schoolfellow and shipmate of mine, and he kindly promised me a passage to Sydney. In respect to Lieutenant Richards and his sub. Tipping, I cannot close this without saying how kind and generous they were; indeed no words can express the gratitude that I have for all they did for me.

APPENDIX.

NOTES ON NEW IRELAND.

(1.) OF New Ireland I had intended to speak more fully, but when I came to condense what I know of this most interesting place I found that in reality I know but very little about it, and even that little I am not at all sure in my own mind is properly authenticated. However, there are a few things that there can be no doubt about, and one of these is, that they are cannibals. It is, of course, very difficult to say positively what may have been the origin of cannibalism, but as far as I can judge, and the native statements seem to bear it out, one of the causes of it is, that at one time these islands were subject to a great drought and famine, and it was then that, in order to maintain life, cannibalism was resorted to: this sounds plausible. Moreover, in New Guinea but very few tribes are known to practise it, and those that do are, I believe, only to be found on the Gulf of Papua, and are undoubtedly the lowest races in New Guinea so far as known at present. It is probable, therefore, that they may have learnt the practice from the natives of the York Peninsula, North Australia, with whom I have little doubt they at one time had considerable intercourse - besides, it is very much despised by other tribes.

It would be a very improbable thing that a drought would affect the whole of New Guinea, and therefore the natives in that part, affected by the famine, would be able either to buy provisions from those not so afflicted, or to go and pillage for it—at any rate they would be able to sustain life without resorting to cannibalism. Of course in Australia things are very different: there never is food enough in one single place to support a tribe, therefore they are nomads; and should a drought occur in their district, all the animals, on which they mainly depend for subsistence, disappear from that part, and leave them no other means of living but by cannibalism; or, again, in order to obtain the necessary animal food, they have to travel until they find some part unaffected by the drought. Here also other tribes have assembled for the same cause; they immediately fight for the right of hunting, and being famished with hunger eat the bodies of their victims.

It no doubt originated also in some cases in the ungovernable hatred and feeling of revenge of one man against another. Not content with killing him, he proceeds to eat his "tongue and heart,"[1] and to smear himself with the kidney fat. This *may* have been so in some few instances, no doubt, but the former cause seems the most likely.

It is not therefore improbable that in comparatively small islands like New Britain and New Ireland drought was the origin, and once having begun this terrible practice revenge kept it up. Moreover, I can state, on the authority of a cannibal chief, that having once indulged in the frightful repast it is very difficult to leave it off. He explained it by saying that "Human flesh was better than pig, turtle, fish, or fowls; and that white men were fools and did not know what was good."

(2.) In New Ireland, on the death of any member of a well-to-do family, one of the men of the same family goes to

---

[1] This expression is made use of in parts of Australia at the present day, and would seem to mean that the heart was eaten to show contempt, and the tongue because of the things spoken against the eater. The kidney fat is to obtain the strength of the victim in addition to his own.

the bush tribe that live in the Rossel Mountains, and obtains
a carved chalk figure, of either a man or a woman according to the sex of the deceased, with which he returns to
his village and with great secrecy gives it to a chief whose
particular business it is to receive it. It is then placed in
a small " mortuary chapel " * (I hardly know what else to
call it) that is built inside another house, and is decorated
with all manner of variegated plants, in company with other
figures of the same description, where it remains (for how
long I do not know). This curious practice arises out of a
superstition with respect to the spirit of the departed, in
which they believe that the ghost must have some habita-
tion on earth, or it will haunt the survivors of its late
family, to work them some mischief; they therefore place
this figure for the spirit to go to, as its late tenement is
decomposed in the earth or sea, according to the place of
burial. Women are never allowed to go near or look upon
these figures, it being death for them to do so.

The chalk of which these figures are composed, and which
is found at the top of the Rossel Mountains, is, I believe, one
of the only, if not the sole deposit of chalk formed in the
South Pacific.

(3.) There is a very curious habit in New Ireland of
placing a young girl on her attaining a marriageable age
in a sort of cage built within the house where she is living,
wreaths of scented herbs being bound round her waist and
neck. The cage is generally built with two floors, and it is
on the upper one that the young lady resides. Being very
small there is only room for her to lie down or sit, but not
sufficient to stand up in; the lower floor is occupied by
either an old woman or a little child. This lasts for about
a month, the young lady only being allowed out of her
somewhat uncomfortable dwelling at night time. It is
impossible to say what the meaning of this custom is.
Some have told me that it is to honour her attaining
womanhood, in the same sense that we make a feast, &c., on

a man attaining his majority. But be this as it may, I am of opinion there is something else behind which I have never been able to discover.

(4.) The New Ireland money is quite of a different character to that of New Britain, as it is formed of a small bivalve shell, of which a number are pierced and strung on a piece of twine, being chipped until quite small, when they are rubbed smooth and circular with pumice-stone; these strings of money measure for one length from nipple to nipple on a man's breast, and are of a yellowy pink colour. Ten lengths are the price of a fair-sized pig.

(5.) The women in New Ireland have a small dress composed of grass, worn both before and behind, which is stained a bright red colour and kept in place by a plaited string round the waist, that is tied just above the hip on one side. The men are naked, as in New Britain.

(6.) The implements of war in New Ireland are much the same as those used in Duke of York, which have been described.

(7.) There is little doubt in my own mind that the inhabitants of New Ireland are the same race of people as those of Gazelle Peninsula in New Britain, as their language is somewhat similar, as will be seen by the vocabulary at the end, but are not the same race as those of Spacious Bay or those from Open Bay to the West. They are also similar to the natives of the Solomon Islands.

(8.) When burying their dead the New Britain natives generally place those of little note in a sitting posture on a reef at low water, where they will on the tide rising be taken away by the sharks, but often they are put into a canoe and placed under ground. When a chief dies his body is laid out in his canoe with scented herbs lying on him, his nearest kin then make a great feast and invite all the neighbouring chiefs and tribes, upon which occasion they present to each visitor a fathom of taboo or shell money, after which the body is covered with cocoa-nut mats and raised up to its resting-place on the forked branches of two trees; then the dancing begins, and is kept up with great vigour all night by the light of blazing fires, and for several nights in succession, drums being beaten in accompaniment to the singing of the dancers. In "singing" they do not use words, but merely sounds.

The talking man of the late chief goes round to each visitor and proclaims his many virtues. The feasting and dancing is generally terminated by something being thrown violently out of the dead chief's canoe into the assembled crowd; the one whom it hits is said to be sure to die soon. After some time the canoe is taken down and buried, but in some districts the succeeding chief, who is the eldest son of the eldest sister of the deceased, takes the head, wrapped in banana leaves, and places it in his hut.

(9.) New Britain wives are always held responsible for anything that is lost or stolen from the house, not the actual thief, as the natives say with some show of sense, that they cannot have been looking out properly or it would not have happened. Women are never entrusted with any secret, as there is a proverb amongst them that "a woman's tongue is hung with a double joint."

(10.) Torches for fishing at night or travelling through the bush are made of dried cocoa-nut leaves tied together.

(11.) In the villages of New Britain the strictest sanitary laws prevail. All offal is removed by the women, and either thrown into the sea, or if in the bush buried some distance away. All market places and cleared spaces in a village are swept every day in order to clear them of dead leaves, sticks, &c., which might hurt the feet of the dancers or harbour insects.

(12.) In New Britain, Duke of York, as well as New Ireland, there is a method of talking when they do not wish to be understood by any stranger. It appears to be a different dialect at each place, but it is common in this, that it is chanted in a sort of falsetto voice, and is apparently cut up into a rough kind of rhythm, in which all the smaller words are left out, and is extremely difficult to understand.

(13.) The names of New Britain men are generally taken from some animal or trees, such as "Aukin," a wallaby, or "Dewai," wood—more generally they are called after some relation or chief; but though the derivations of the names are often difficult to trace, they are nearly always corruptions of the name of something strong, active, or grand. There are exceptions, as for instance the name of a chief at Kubakadaie, "Tor Long Long," "Tor" signifying chief or Mr., and "Long Long" fool, though I should have said he was anything but that. I therefore surmise that there has been very probably two meanings to "Long Long," in the same way that there is in the expression, "Don't make an *ass* of yourself," or "Don't be a *goose*," but which second meaning has been dropped, as in the case of our English names "Smith," "Whitehead;" and here we do not expect to see a blacksmith or any kind of smith in trade, neither do we necessarily expect to see a gentleman with white hair when Mr. Whitehead is announced. It is, as I said before, difficult to discover the meaning or derivation of many names, but there can be no doubt that they arose originally from some act or thing associated with the man's life.

Sometimes it is from some expression of the mother's; perhaps she says, " He is as strong as a young tree," or " as straight as a bamboo," or, again, " as heavy as a stone."   He will then be called either " young tree," " bamboo," or " stone."   In the case of the women the same arguments apply, except that they are generally named after flowers, birds, or butterflies.

(14.) The natives of New Britain, as well as those of Duke of York and New Ireland, would put to shame most people in Europe in their wonderful knowledge of natural history. There is no beast, bird, reptile, fish, or insect of which they do not know the distinctive name as well as that applying to the class to which it belongs, having also a general term for the whole species.   For instance, take a caterpillar; you ask a native what its name is, he will tell you, " It is a caterpillar, changing to a moth, a tree-borer, a cocoon spinner."   Or a beetle, that " It is a beetle, larva eats offal, nymph buries in the earth."   He will give you all this information as though it were one name.   In the case of an animal, say a flying squirrel—" It is a Dirra-dirra " (the sound it makes), " lives on fruit, springs from tree to tree at night, and brings forth its young."   Even the young lads seem to know the name of the smallest insect; but if they should happen to be asked one that they do not know they turn to the nearest man, who at once supplies the information.

(15.) There is one kind of animal in New Britain that has always baffled me—it is a creature that shows a most brilliant phosphorescent light at night, and which is generally to be found in an old tree.   I have tried to approach it, but on coming within a few yards of it its light disappears.   I have hunted the spot where it was seen without success; I have tried shooting it both with shot, as well as a piece of chalk, to mark the exact spot, but always

without success, and have had to give it up in despair. The
natives are very frightened of it, and call it "Toberan-
quarburra." I can only account for this curious phenomenon
by supposing it to be either a phosphorescent beetle or
lizard; the natives know nothing whatever as to its origin.

(16.) It is the custom in New Britain to blacken the
teeth; this is done on a youth's attaining man's estate, and
although the teeth have already been much discoloured by
the process of chewing betel-nut, it is considered the correct
thing to stain them with the juice of a certain plant that
makes them perfectly black; this is not necessary for women,
but their teeth become black by chewing betel-nut in
course of time. In fact the mouth of a New Britain man or
woman is not a pleasant sight at any time, for the juice of
the betel-nut always clings to their lips and gives an
appearance as of constantly spitting blood. It is, however, a
considerable breach of etiquette not to partake of it when
offered.

(17.) In the New Britain language there are some words
that bear a curious affinity to those of civilised or other
nations; for instance, take the native word "a pup,"
meaning a dog. This would be easily accounted for were
dogs not indigenous to these islands, as for instance in the
Mortlock Islands, where they were introduced only a few
years ago. When the natives first saw dogs they heard the
sailors call them, saying, "Come here!" "Come here!" and
dogs in these islands have since gone by the name of a
"Come-yere." But dogs are as indigenous to New Britain as
dingoes are to Australia, there being but one breed common
to both New Ireland and New Britain, and they are unable
to bark; I cannot therefore account for it except as a curious
coincidence.

(18.) I have come to the conclusion that in these islands
one of the most primitive forms of language is to be found.
Protected as they are from the Malay Archipelago by the

great barrier of New Guinea, and far enough removed from the Polynesian and Micronesian groups as to have been practically inaccessible from them, they can therefore have had little intercourse with any outsiders, save from the north-east coast of New Guinea on one side and the Solomon Islands on the other, both of which are comparatively unknown and equally primitive places, though not so inaccessible, owing to their lying closer to the other islands of the Pacific, and consequently not so likely to have retained in its purity the language of their first ancestors. I therefore here take the opportunity of comparing the method of counting in these islands with some of the more ancient forms of figures extant; I do not claim that their manner of counting is at all peculiar to these people, for that would be absurd, knowing as we do that all savage races make use of the hands and feet for the purpose; but I do contend that here it is their own, not introduced from elsewhere, and therefore may be considered as primitive and not an improvement on a still earlier form, the necessity to find a system for counting having occurred, of which this was the immediate and since unaltered result.

Let us now take the word " five "; it is in New Britain " à lima," this being the word for a hand. Dr. Tylor tells us in his Anthropology that this is also the case with the Tamanacs of the Orinoco, as well as in other places in a less direct manner. He also gives us the old Malay word (precisely the same) " lima," which now is used as the word five, but formerly meant hand. Moreover, the word is common to the whole of Melanesia, still signifying five, though in many cases the meaning " hand " has been dropped, as in the case of the Malays, which would seem to suggest their being of common descent. The New Britain counting begins with the little finger of the left hand, and so on to the thumb, calling each finger by name: this begins again on the right hand, only each finger is called the pair of the corresponding finger on the left hand, thus : left hand, tikai (little finger), urua (third finger), otul (second finger), ivat (first finger), à lima (thumb); right hand, lip tikai (little finger), lov-urua (third finger), lov-otule (second finger), (lov-ivat (first finger), tur à lim (thumb).   Taking one instance, the first finger of the left hand, corresponding to four with us, is "ivat," and the same finger on the right

Fig 1.

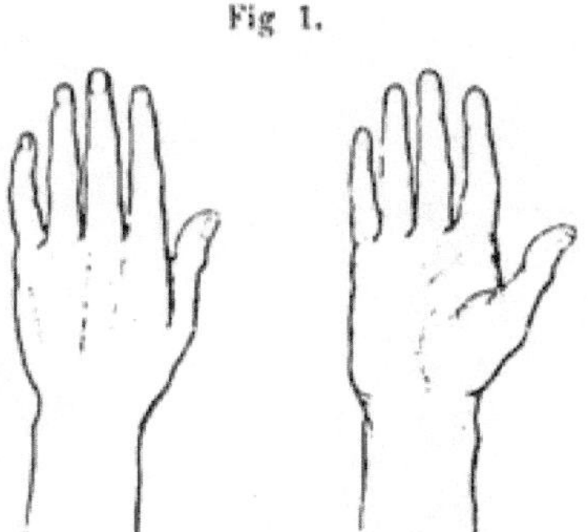

NEW BRITAIN—TUR A LIM, SIGNIFYING TEN SEPARATE ARTICLES.

hand, which would correspond to our nine, "lov-ivat," is simply the pair of four, which with us would be eight, but is in reality nine; tur à lima—or short, tur à lim—means ten separate articles (Fig. 1); ten in a bunch is avo nun, or

Fig. 2.

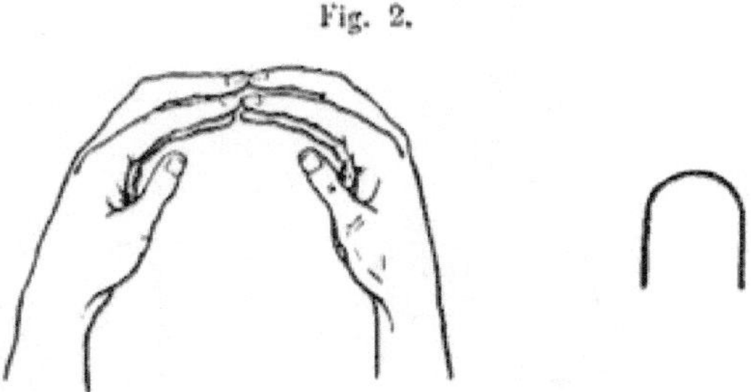

ANCIENT EGYPTIAN TEN.

both hands together, the fingers interlaced.   The word " urua tan-ivat," the New Britain for twenty, is made up from the elementary numbers two, four, and five, urua, ivat, and à lim; the latter number being understood in ordinary conversation.   The composition of the word being " two sets (of things, in which two sets, together there are) four fives;" so that the whole would read urua, two; tan, sets; ivat, four; à lim, five.

Dr. Tylor again, in his excellent little work, which I might almost call the handbook of Anthropology, tells us

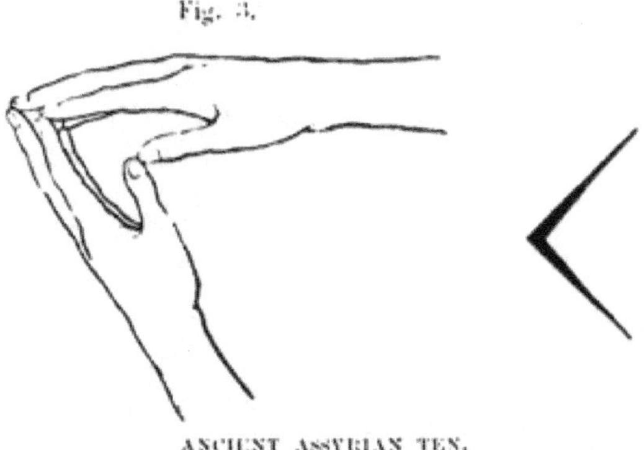

ANCIENT ASSYRIAN TEN.

that there is ineffaceable proof that the numerals arose out of the primitive counting on fingers and toes. Let us first take two instances of characters which he gives in his book—ancient Egyptian first. The ten here is in the form of a Roman arch (Figure 2); here one can surely trace two hands

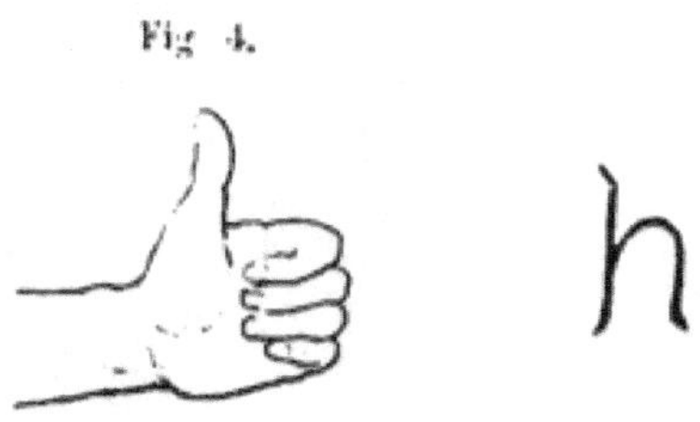

ANCIENT ARABIC FIVE.

together, the tips of the fingers touching, as may be seen at the present time amongst some tribes of Melanesia when expressing ten. Again, take ancient Assyrian (Figure 3): this also expresses ten. Here are the two hands again, as may be seen in some tribes of Melanesia with the hands together, fingers extended in front of the body. In ancient Arabic five is represented thus (Figure 4). Here again, though perhaps more obscure, is the closed fist of the left hand,

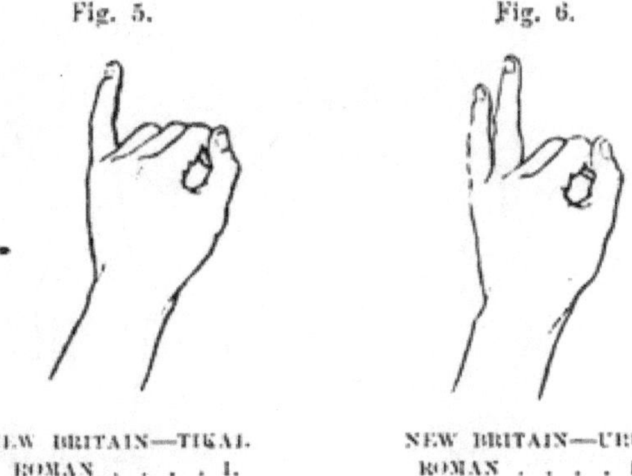

thumb extended, and it is from this numeral that our "5" is obtained.

Take another instance, the old Roman numerals, I., II., III.,

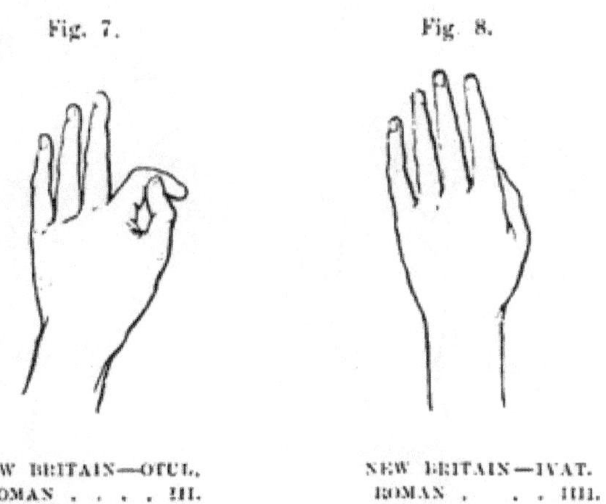

IIII., V., VI., VII., VIII., VIIII., X. (Figs. 5–14). Here may be seen the whole of the fingers of each hand, "one" corresponding to the little finger of the left hand, and so on until five, which is represented as our "v.," and no doubt was taken from the

v shape of the thumb when extended with all the fingers touching (Figure 9). The numerals were then continued by adding to the v on the left hand the fingers of the right

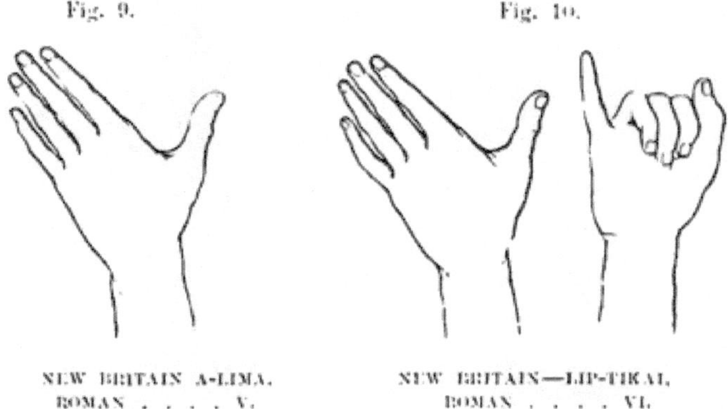

in succession until ten is reached, when the two hands were clasped together, fingers interlaced, from which arose the x (Figure 14). This seems very conclusive, and I have little

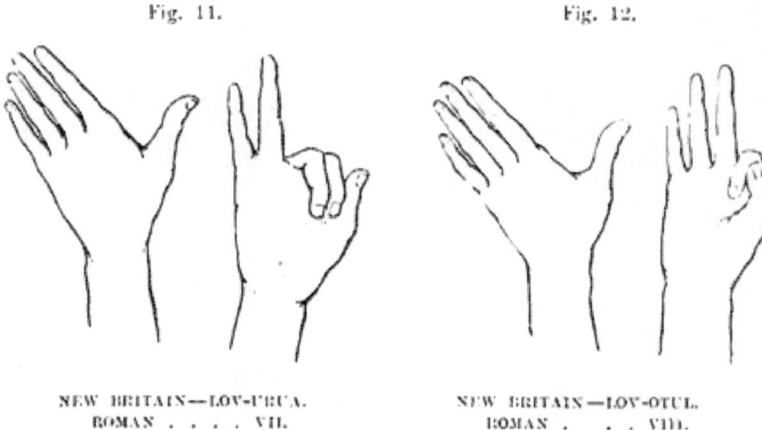

doubt that in future times had these people of New Britain been left to develop, unaffected by external influence, that their numerals would have assumed a form similar to these, other tribes of the same race adopting other forms, but the same fundamental method of numeration.

I cannot enter fully into the subject here, but I have little doubt that the numbers of every ancient, and therefore modern, nation may be traced to the one origin. No doubt it is a subject that has been fully worked out before, but I cannot help introducing it here, and by this means, in some small degree, connecting the present with the ancient savage.

In counting days or moons, or even numbers of bunches of cocoa-nuts, &c., these natives always use a piece of twine or

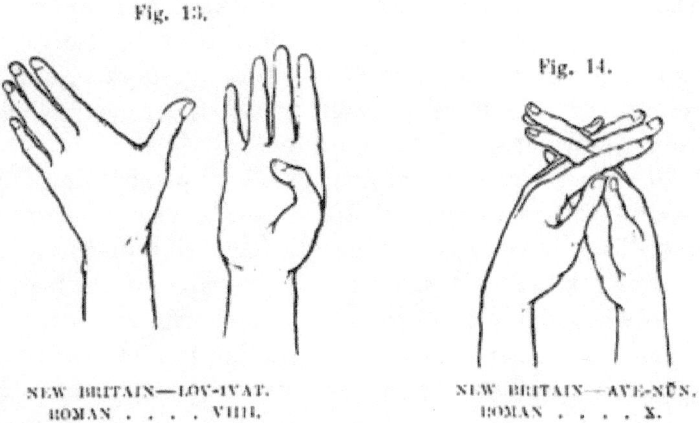

bark, in which they place the requisite number of knots. I observed an improvement on this at one place to the westward, which was a necklace made with ten twine pendants on which were worked a number of movable Turk's-head knots. If wishing to remember the number of anything it was only necessary to slide the requisite number of knots to the upper part of the pendant next the throat, where they would be kept in place by a small slipknot tied in the twine below them : this shows that advance of culture is even now taking place amongst these islanders.

(19.) It is to my mind worthy of notice how phonetic the

language in these islands is—instance Rok-rok, a frog. This is the exact imitation of the sound produced by the frog, and when some thousands of them are all croaking together, one can shut one's eyes and fancy oneself in a boiler factory, or on board a ship, where a large number of hands have been turned on to caulk the deck.

Câka-ru-ku, a fowl, is also a good imitation of the cry peculiar to that bird. There are also sounds of comparison, if I may call them so; thus, ai-āp is New Britain for fire; it also signifies quickness in movement; thus one would say, " Nakabea Ai-āp Ai-āp " (" Give me fire quickly "). This is undoubtedly taken from the rapidity with which fire moves, although there is the word " Alūt," also signifying quickness; they are sometimes used together, but Ai-āp is always used as the superlative, thus: " Nu-on-ati alūt pumpum Ai-āp "— literally, " Come quick, quicker, quickest," or corresponding to our " Come as quick as lightning."

(20.) There are some curious laws about prostitution. Any woman who has no relations living can become a prostitute, but will not have to be avenged by her tribe in the case of her being killed. If any man should afterwards take her for a wife, she will then have equal rights with other women. It is not considered degrading to a woman to be a prostitute, except so far as her not having any one to care for her. No woman that has a father or mother living can become one unless by their consent, but this is often given. If, however, she becomes one without their consent she is liable to be killed by any of her relations, as she was probably intended as a wife for a man in some particular family, or it may have been that she had been bought as wife for a chief. There is a drum beaten on certain nights for all prostitutes to go out into the bush, where they are chased by the young unmarried men. This is called " Lu-Lu," a term applied to the women themselves, or to anything connected with the custom. I believe, but am not certain, that any children that may be the result of this are killed; I cannot feel sure about it as I could never get any one to tell me that I could rely upon, but I think their reticence goes a considerable way towards proving this to be a fact, for were it not so there would be no cause for silence.

(21.) With respect to the so much vexed question of the murders of white men by natives in the South Sea Islands, I am of opinion that it arises from two causes. First, though not perhaps as much as some people state, by acts of violence by white men on the natives, who retaliate, either against the offender, or the next white man that comes to the spot; and secondly, from the incontrollable avarice of the natives, augmented in many cases by returned labour from Australia. In the first case I have little doubt, from my own observations, substantiated by statements made by natives themselves, and by careful inquiry amongst the white traders as well as missionaries, that these abuses by whites have been much exaggerated. I am not in any way wishing to exonerate or shield those that are to blame, but to give a fair and impartial view of the facts of the case. Undoubtedly cases have occurred, and I fear that they have been far from few, but are not to be compared in number with those committed by natives on white men. Take the case of Bishop Paterson or of Captain Goodenough; I take these cases simply because they are better known. It has been stated in each of these that they were murdered out of retaliation for the depredations of some trader who had been at the same places previously. When the authority of this statement is examined it falls to the ground, as it appears that no one can say in either case who or what trader it was, and if they cannot tell this how can they say that such was the case?

Now let us take the character of natives as a rule, and not only their character but their education. In character they are avaricious to the last degree, they are also treacherous, and the passion for killing is often so strong in them that I have been told by natives themselves not to walk in front of them when they were armed, lest this feeling should get the better of them, and they might do me an injury. Of course this is not so strong a feeling with some as with others, but I believe it to be more or less natural to all, especially the wilder and more savage tribes. Moreover, from infancy they have been brought up to carrying arms and to consider every stranger as an enemy, either openly or covertly. A man without arms they despise and look down upon as being no warrior, and if he be a stranger all the more do their feelings rise against him. They know no better, and the difficulty seems to be with civilized people that they cannot place themselves in imagination in the position of one of these natives; could they do this they would understand their nature better, and there would be less nonsense talked about the poor ignorant savage, the victim of the designing trader.

As for the trader himself the idea seems very general that he goes from place to place carrying war and bloodshed with him. Now, in the name of common sense, which is the most likely to benefit the trader, to be always imposing upon and cheating these people, and by this means bringing about such strife and contention that it is not safe for him to trade there any more, or by friendly and fair means to obtain goods that anyhow he will make enormous profit out of, and thus not risk his own life and the lives of those with him, but continue to trade on friendly terms wherever he goes? I am fully aware that many quarrels arise from misunderstandings perhaps of the language, or a mistake as to intention, but I maintain that in nine cases out of ten it is the native who takes the aggressive, not the trader.

Again, there is in Australia what is called the labour trade. Vessels go round the different islands having on board a Government agent; they obtain a number of young men by agreement with the chiefs or the men themselves to come to Australia to work at the plantations for three years. They go, and in three years' time are returned to their native island; they have been just long enough with whites to learn a lot of roguery, and they also pick up a little knowledge about ships from their return voyage. They are paid off from their late employers with clothes, knives, beads, and perhaps a musket, powder and shot; they land on their island, and all their friends come round and see what they have got; then the explanation follows that white men have plenty of these things in their ships; avarice is at once aroused, and perhaps the next ship that calls at that place is made the subject of an attack, the lately returned labour (as they are called) giving advice as to how success can be best obtained, for which their previous knowledge duly qualifies them. Perhaps they succeed only too well, and they attempt the same thing another time and most likely succeed again; other tribes hear of it and are equally anxious to try their hand. A man-of-war is sent down, all the natives decamp into the bush inland, and a few houses are burnt (which perhaps is rather a charity than otherwise, for sanitary reasons). Possibly Johnny or Jacky, who can talk a little English and knows a great deal of roguery, is captured and tells a sad story of how the white men carried off the women, &c. He knows enough of white men and has heard sufficient of a man-of-war to know this story will go down; he is rewarded by having a shirt and tobacco given him, and is told to go and tell his people not to attack white men's vessels, and he goes off to his tribe laughing in his sleeve (if he had one) and thinking what fools these white men are, which opinion is fully echoed by the remainder of his tribe.

It often occurs that the women are used as decoys instead of being carried off in the ruthless manner described by some people. I know of a case that is well authenticated where the chief offered the captain his daughter to be his woman. The captain, no doubt thinking to augment his friendly relations and increase his trade, accepted; a few days afterwards he and nearly all his crew were brutally murdered, a few escaping in a boat, the captain being struck down by the very woman the chief had given him to wife. I am not defending the morality of the captain's proceeding; I merely wish to show that this was a preconcerted plan to plunder the vessel.

Another case, that of a well-known man who was

murdered with his wife and child and the whole of his
crew simply for the sake of plundering the vessel. He had
been trading for many years in these seas, and was always
considered a most upright man and very friendly with all
natives with whom he had any dealings. When the news
of his death was brought to another island where he was
known, a chief came running to the missionary's house to
know if it was true, and when he heard that it was, his
grief was ungovernable, he beat his head on the ground and
cried out that he wanted to go and fight the murderers and
eat them all up. asking if it was far off, and begging the
missionary to get a ship and take him and his fighting
men to the place, that they might avenge his death. This
would not seem to show that the trader was otherwise
than a friend to natives. I could tell of many other such
cases—hundreds I might almost say.

But, again, there have been and undoubtedly are bad men
who trade in these islands, and who think very little of
committing any outrage on natives; but these men, I am
glad to say, are getting fewer every year, and their acts of
violence are more often directed against other traders than
against the natives themselves (I shall give an instance of
this further on); but such acts in themselves set a terrible
example, that the natives are only too ready to profit by.
But, as I said before, such men as perpetrate these crimes
are getting scarce, thanks to the action of the Government
in sending men-of-war cruisers to these seas. Even in
the case of an outrage—carrying off a woman, or even kid-
napping a number of natives, which is almost impossible
now—I hope I shall not be misunderstood when I say
that the natives do not keep their resentment, or indeed
do not have so much resentment against the perpetrators
as we civilised people would be inclined to imagine. In
the first place, their lives are passed in one constant state
of defence against or aggression on other tribes; they lose
many men and women in their own wars, by ambush,
treachery, or open fighting; their lives are a continual
round of what we should consider the most horrible sights,

but to which they are accustomed; yet I hold that no punishment is too severe for white men who take advantage of these poor creatures' misfortunes and barbarism to work them harm, to say nothing of the unfortunates that they kidnap, who may be benefited by the result, but most likely are not. What I wish to explain by this statement is, that the argument so often made use of to prove that a murder was caused by an outrage formerly committed is generally an exaggeration.

In a case where a quarrel arises over some trading transaction, and when the natives and whites both get angry, spears and bullets are exchanged, and it might be considered unsafe for a man to venture on shore at this time; but a case of this sort has occurred to me, when I landed at the very spot where a man had been shot in an affair of this description and they were actually holding the funeral obsequies of the dead man at the time—though of this I was not aware until I reached the village—yet no man lifted a hand to do me any harm; and, so far as I could learn from the natives, the fray was owing to the duplicity of a chief who had stolen some trade and had not payed for it in copra. This led to a dispute, and the natives had thrown spears, which had been answered by shots from the traders' boat; and this man had unfortunately been shot, yet I did not hear a word mentioned about revenge. I also am fully persuaded that the chiefs care more for the trade that the white men bring in the course of business than for the death of a good many of their own people. Thus I have come to these two conclusions: first, that the labour trade is strongly to be condemned as far as the South Seas are concerned, and also that the trader is more often sinned against than sinning.

In saying this I allude more particularly to the New Hebrides, Santa Cruz, Soloman, New Ireland and New Britain, though I am glad to say the two latter have been so far comparatively free from labour trade. Whilst making these remarks on this subject I may state that my observations extended over a period of nearly seven years;

and I can conscientiously say that I have endeavoured to get as near the right solution of this question as possible without bias, and feel sure that if the natives were brought to see that it was more to their interest to be friendly, by receiving a swift punishment for the unprovoked attacks on trading vessels, that in a short time no more outrages would be heard of on their side; at the same time let there be an equally swift punishment for any white man against whom it can be proved that he has acted in an oppressive or illegal manner against any natives; but by all means let their punishments be real, not fictitious, as they generally have been. This might easily be accomplished had captains of men-of-war cruising in these seas more power given them to act on the spot.

"Severity," as Dr. Johnson said, "is the way to govern men, yet is not the way to mend them;" but in this case they require governing before it is possible to mend them. There is one more thing I would urge: that the languages spoken by these natives should be collected as far as possible, and that a book in which they are collectively printed should be placed at the disposal of the captains of men-of-war cruising among these islands, in order that they may be less at the mercy of a one-sided interpreter. This would be an immense help to justice and trade, as well as of equal value to the scientific world, and would not be so hard to obtain as might be imagined.

I now will give a short account of a case that occurred in these islands that came under my immediate knowledge, but which I am very thankful to say was not enacted by Englishmen. I omit names for obvious reasons.

A few years ago there was in Cambria, New Britain, a trader whom we will call J——. He was trading for a German firm, having signed an agreement to do so with the firm's accredited agent in these parts, whose name shall be Captain L——. J—— had been trading in this spot but a short time when he was foully murdered by the natives, but his wife (a Samoan woman) was taken on board Captain L——'s vessel. It was even then rumoured amongst the few whites who

were at that time near the place that Captain L—— had
something to do with the murder, as he took no notice of the
theft of a large quantity of trade goods which were stolen
from J——'s house at the time of his murder; and, although
knowing well who the culprits were, never demanded their
restitution, or took any notice of the crime committed. A
year or so later one of Captain L——'s traders, a half-caste,
to be called in future K——, murdered another trader of the
same firm in these islands, in a boat, by beating him to death
with the stone ballast, whilst in a state of intoxication; but
for this K—— was not punished in any way by Captain
L——, but was still employed as trader, for Captain L——'s
own purposes. A little later an English seaman that had been
on board Captain L——'s vessel was missing, Captain L——
himself making all sorts of anxious inquiries about him
amongst the natives and other white men, missionaries, &c.,
as to whether they had seen or heard anything of him. It
afterwards transpired from natives and others that this seaman had some earrings that Captain L——'s Samoan wife was
anxious to buy. On Christmas Eve it appears that Captain
L—— gave his men several bottles of spirits to keep Christmas with, by which means the crew were rendered more or less
intoxicated. It was then that the before-mentioned seaman
went aft to Captain L——'s wife, and offered her the earrings
on condition that she consented to certain improper proposals
he made her; she told this to Captain L——, who ran up and
knocked the man down with an iron belaying-pin; the seaman, on recovering his senses, drew an unloaded revolver,
and in his drunken state threatened to shoot Captain L——,
whereupon he was knocked down again from behind by one
of the mates. When he recovered the second time he was
told to go on shore, which he did, having been somewhat
sobered by the rough treatment he had received. As soon as
he was gone Captain L—— sent K—— with a message to
certain chiefs on shore that this seaman was to be murdered,
and that he would pay them when it was done. This, by their
own confession, these chiefs accomplished only too well,
taking the body out to sea in a canoe with a heavy stone

attached, and sinking it   After some months a man-of-war schooner arrived at Duke of York, K—— having been in the meantime placed on a new station in New Ireland; but, coming over to Duke of York for some medicine from the mission, and hearing that an English man-of-war was there, he was frightened in consequence of his having murdered the trader, as before stated, and turned back. Captain L—— however heard that he had been over, and also believing that he had been to the man-of-war, came to his station and accused him of it, saying, "You have been carrying stories of me to the man-of-war;" and, when K—— said he had not, told him he "lied." Captain L—— then said, "I want to ask you a question: what do you know about J——? K—— answered, "I do not know much." "Then," said Captain L——, "what do you know about, the English seaman?" (mentioning his name). K—— answered, getting angry, "I know you paid the natives to kill him." "Very well," said Captain L——, "I will stop your telling any more tales about me." He then seized up a loaded musket that was standing near, with the intention of shooting K——; but K—— was too quick for him, and wrenched it out of his hand; and in the scuffle that ensued Captain L—— pushed K—— out of the house, and shut the door. K——, having the rifle in his hand, fired through the door at Captain L——, who was standing against it, and shot him dead.

Some of this was gathered from the natives, and the rest was told by K—— when a prisoner. I have met other captains of the same firm, and never wish to meet more gentlemanly, pleasant men. This account needs no comment; but I am thankful to say that such cases are very rare, yet where they have existed the example to natives is a terrible one. Though in this instance I am inclined to think that the natives who took part in it were fully impressed by the sequel, as also by the arrest of K——, to assist in any such thing again.

(22.) There is a fact well worth mentioning with respect to carrying dogs on board a vessel in these parts otherwise

than the mere fact of their use as a watch. It is that they
are very sensitive of an approach of land or reefs; and I
found that whenever our dogs began to sniff over the side
it was a sure sign of there being a reef not far off; and not
only that, but they will continue to do this until the danger
is a long way off. They will detect the smell of a reef even
at night whilst asleep, and will awake and run to the side
of the vessel and whine, so that they are of as much use
as a lead is in other places, for many reefs here are so steep
to, that the lead is no guide.

[From the *Proceedings of the Zoological Society of London,*
June 15, 1880.]

'Field Notes on the Morroop (*Casuarius bennetti*) of New
Britain,' by WILFRED POWELL.

The interior of the northern peninsula of New Britain is
composed of high table-land and grassy plains of considerable
area. It is on these plains that the cassowary of this
island (*Casuarius bennetti*) is mostly to be found. These
birds are generally seen moving slowly along in the high
grass, with their heads just showing above it. The plains
appear to be their feeding ground, as they are rarely seen
in the bush during the day-time. They are gregarious in
their habits, travelling in flocks of three or four; I have
sometimes seen as many as seven in a flock together.
When in motion they always go in Indian file, with the cock
bird leading. They do not seem to advance over the
ground very quickly unless alarmed, when they travel with
marvellous rapidity, having a bounding motion, which is
not, in my estimation, very graceful. When they select a
place for their nests they do so usually in an open glade
that is well timbered, but without underscrub. Here they
scrape the earth together into a slight heap, with a depres-
sion in the centre. The nest is circular in form, about five
feet in diameter, the outside being raised about six inches
from the ground level. Here they lay their eggs, which

are left to hatch by the heat of the sun. The natives, who search for these nests, in order to obtain the eggs for food (which they consider a great delicacy, though I cannot say I like them myself, their flavour being too strong), assure me that they seldom find more than three at a time in one nest, and that when the bird has laid one egg, it leaves the nest for some days before returning to lay another; whether they lay eggs elsewhere in the meanwhile I cannot say. The egg is about five inches long by three inches wide at the broadest part, and is thickly mottled with delicate little green spots.

The cassowary's food consists of lizards, frogs, fruits, nuts, and it is also very fond of fish. Whilst in conversation with a native one day, he told me that the pook-pook (or crocodile) was very fond of cassowary's flesh, and often eats them. It puzzled me very much to understand how it was that the crocodile, who is so unwieldy in his movements on shore, could possibly catch a bird of such swiftness. It chanced that afterwards I witnessed an interesting occurrence that may very possibly account for it. I was one day some little distance up a river in New Britain, sitting in my little dingy, fishing (the boat and myself being practically hidden by bushes); I saw a morroop (cassowary) come down to the water's edge, and stand for some minutes apparently watching the water carefully; it then stepped into the river where the water was about three feet deep, and, partially squatting down, spread its wings out, submerging them, the feathers being spread and ruffled. The bird remained perfectly motionless; I also noticed that the eyes were closed as if asleep. It remained in this position for fully a quarter of an hour, when, suddenly closing its wings and straightening its feathers, it stepped out on to the bank, where, shaking itself several times, a quantity of small fishes fell from under the wings and from amidst the feathers, which were immediately picked up and swallowed. The fishes had evidently mistaken the feathers for a description of weed that grows in the water along the banks of the rivers in this island, and very much resembles the feathers of the cassowary, and in which the smaller fish hide to avoid the larger ones that prey on them. I think it would have been very easy for a crocodile to seize the bird whilst thus in the water. These birds generally go into the thickest scrubs to sleep; and, although I have never myself seen them, I heard from the natives that the hen birds sleep with their heads under their wings, lying down, and that the male bird lies with his head stretched out along the ground, probably to guard against surprise.

The method the natives adopt to catch them is to light fires in a large circle of about a mile in circumference in the long grass on the plains, leaving one opening in the circle at which are stationed several men armed with spears. The fire is made to burn towards the centre of the circle by men and women on the outside, who beat out with bushes all fire likely to spread in any other direction; this drives the cassowaries that are within the circle to the opening, where they are speared by the men stationed there for that purpose. Another method is to place a rope (made of thé bark of a tree), with a running noose at one end and a loop at the other; round the nest, covering it with sand so as to hide it. The native takes the other end (which has been wound round his body) behind a tree, and waits for the bird to come. When she is seated on the nest in the act of laying an egg, he pulls the rope, and the noose catches the legs of the cassowary; he then runs with the other end to a tree, and takes a round turn, which holds the bird in its struggle to escape until it is quite tired out and helpless; he then despatches it with his spear. One man, when I was in the Goonun district (New Britain), met with his death in the following peculiar manner, whilst waiting for a cassowary to come to its nest. Having his rope already laid, he fell asleep; in the meanwhile the bird came to its nest and laid its egg, but, when going away, got one of its legs entangled in the noose. Thus the man who had the rope wound round his body was dragged along the ground, and, I suppose, struck against a tree, which stunned or killed him. Both the body of the man and the bird were found dead some days afterwards, still fastened together with the rope, at some considerable distance from the nest.

The bones of the cassowary are used in many ways by the natives, the leg-bones being prized to put on the butt ends of spears to balance them; others of the bones are used for spatulas, knives, &c. The feathers are made into head-dresses and brushes for driving flies away. The sharp-pointed claws from the toe are in one part of New Britain used for points of spears, and are fastened on with wax, which when the spear is imbedded in the body melts, so that when the wooden part of the spear is drawn out the horn point remains in the flesh.

These birds become quite domesticated and tame if kept about a house, and will follow like a dog and feed out of the hand. They have a peculiar cry, beginning high, and coming down the scale about five notes. The natives have adopted this cry as their war cry. The young one makes a whistling noise; also when feeding make a chirping something like a chicken, only considerably louder.

The young on leaving the egg is left to shift for itself, and does not join a flock until it attains maturity; which, the natives tell me, takes about five years. The young bird is far from pretty, being covered with a light brown down, which grows darker as the bird ages, until it reaches the rich black of the full-grown bird. The wings are very small in comparison to its size, having no pinion feathers, but in their place four black spine quills, which the natives prize to wear through the cartilage of the nose. The horny comb on the head of the male bird is used by him for pushing his way through the thick scrub, which is very dense in some places, being often composed of prickly palm or a creeping cane which is covered with sharp thorns, and which would, were it not for the comb, tear the head of the bird.

It is a curious fact that there are no cassowaries in New Ireland, it only being distant from New Britain thirty miles, with Duke of York Island lying between them, which

also has no cassowaries on it. I saw some fossil footprints on
a large flat rock near the shore in New Ireland which
appear to me to be the marks of cassowaries feet, being those
of a large bird with only the three front toes, which, if
they should be cassowaries footprints, tend to show that
they must have been there at one time.

The flesh of the morroop is often eaten by the natives,
and the oil that is extracted from the fat is considered very
valuable as a remedy for rheumatism. Altogether the
cassowary is an extremely useful bird to the natives in
every way, and would form a most interesting study to the
naturalist.

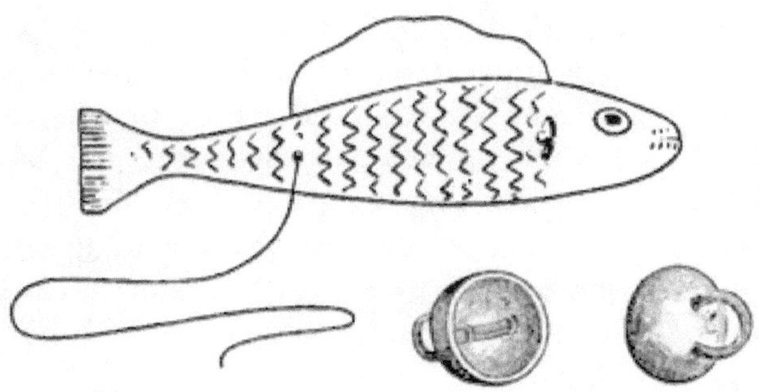

COCOA-NUT SHELLS AND SLIP-NOOSE USED IN CATCHING SHARKS,
NEW BRITAIN.

These natives are excessively clever at catching sharks.
They do it in an altogether novel manner; on looking into a
fishing canoe that is prepared for an expedition one sees a
pair of half-cocoanut shells with plaited twine handles
fastened through two holes at the back; also a piece of strong
but light wood cut in the shape of a fish, about two feet six
inches long, by six inches broad in the widest place; a
strong rope of cane or twisted bark is fastened by a toggle
through a hole near the head, and passes again through a
hole near the tail of this wooden fish, leaving a loop that
may be made any depth by drawing the rope through the
second hole—the rope is perhaps two fathoms in length.
On arriving at the fishing ground a native slips his hand

through the loop at the back of the half-cocoanut shells (as we should a pair of cymbals); these he strikes and rubs together under the water alongside his canoe, whilst another native holds the noose with the wooden fish in readiness. The noise made by the cocoanut shells attracts any shark that may be near, and he comes up close alongside the canoe to see what it is. The native with the noose draws it out to the right size, and quickly slips it over the head and fins, at the same time drawing it tight, and the shark is a prisoner; but it takes some time to tire him out, and he often tows the canoe a long distance before he is finally conquered and killed by spears. The natives say that the noise made by the cocoanut shells is exactly similar to that made by bonita fish when springing out of the water, and it is this attracts the shark; and on coming up he is so anxious and greedy after prey that he is easily caught. Usually the natives are successful, and bring in several sharks, of which they are particularly fond. On the other hand, they often get a canoe broken or upset when tackling a large one, if great skill is not used in its management.

(23.) The legends of these natives are very absurd and impossible as a rule, and one can generally detect a true story from a false one by the absence of exaggeration in the former. If a native wishes to invent a story he dresses it up with the most improbable adjuncts that he can possibly command. One instance will be sufficient to illustrate this. "At one time a woman was delivered of a son, who had such a big head that every one was surprised; he was able to walk and talk as soon as he was born. One day, soon after, his father killed a pig, part of which he hung up to the roof of his house to keep it from the dogs whilst he and his wife went out to work on a yam patch. On returning home he found the piece of pig gone, and he asked his son where it was. He said he didn't know, as he had been asleep most of the time that they had been away. The next day the father hung up some turtle, and on returning this was also gone ; also other natives who had left their huts complained of losing food. This went on for some time, people losing fish, pork, fowls and all manner of food. At last one day the father and another man determined to watch, so they hung up a piece of pork in each house, and the others went away to work at the yams ; but the father and the other man hid themselves where they could see all that was going on. After the others had been gone a little time he saw his baby son get up and shake himself; he then grew up to such a size that his head touched the top of the house, when he seized the piece of pork and swallowed it whole ; he then changed into a lizard, and ran to the other man's dwelling, where he again grew to the top of the house and ate the pork ; then he changed into a rat and went to another house ; and so on. The father and the other man having seen all this, ran to the others and told them, whereupon it was decided to kill the child, which they did, and burnt its body."

Very different to the foregoing however are their stories of a race of men with tails ; also a race of little men represented as being about three feet high—of these their accounts do not vary, and are consistent with what one might suppose to be facts. For instance, these people are not attributed with any supernatural propensities or gifts, but are described as men like other natives, building houses and carrying spears, &c. ; the only thing perhaps at all exaggerated about the story is that they make a hole in the ground with a stick, when they sit down, for the tail to go into, because the tails are unbendable, but even this seems to bear the stamp of truth about it ; for had a native invented the story, he would in all probability have made it a flexible one, as the only other tails that they have any knowledge of are those of the dog, cuscus, wallaby, &c., which of course are flexible ; therefore had this been a mere creation of imagination it would probably have taken some such form as this : " that they had tails which trailed on the ground behind them, and which they swung round them when fighting, like a club." The fact of their tails being stiff inclines me to believe that there has been a family with such an appendage at one time amongst them : indeed it is a well-known thing that there was such a family in Austria. However, although on the coast the natives are quite confident as to where these people are situated, on going to search for them they are always reported to have moved somewhere else.

This story is told word for word the same in New Guinea, which is curious, to say the least of it, though not by the natives of the districts between Spacious and Open Bays, as far as Cape Gloucester. It is confined to the Gazelle Peninsula in New Britain, but is heard of again in New Guinea, some two hundred miles distant. There is no such story in New Ireland.

(24.) In the volcanic portions of New Britain that wonderful builder the megapode (*Megapodius Duskeri*) dispenses with the huge mounds of vegetable matter and earth that it usually accumulates to lay its eggs in—and places them in the cracks and crevices on the sides of an active volcano, where the pumice stone, being superheated by steam and the fire below, supplies the place of the warmth caused by the decaying vegetation.

(25.) It is curious to note how the active volcanoes of New Britain seem to be entirely situated on the northern side of the island. I will take them in rotation: first, " The Mother "—extinct volcano, crater filled with fresh water, two thousand four hundred and seventy feet high ; active volcano immediately below it, with two extinct craters and hot-water spring, all situated on the Blanche Peninsula. Second, New Island, ten feet in height, crater filled with hot salt water ; rose in one night during the eruption of the active volcano on Blanche Peninsula (May 1878). Third, Mount Beautemps Beaupré, one thousand eight hundred feet high—extinct volcano situated in the centre of Gazelle Peninsula. Fourth, Father and Sons—North Son, apparently extinct, one thousand three hundred feet high ; Father, active, four thousand feet high ; South Son, active, three thousand feet high. Fifth, Duportail Island—active, one thousand feet. Sixth, numerous small volcanic craters, apparently extinct, along the coast between Low Point and Hummock Head. Seventh, Island Point and Two Peak Mountain—extinct. Eighth, Willaumez, Raoul, Gicquel and Du Faure Islands—apparently extinct; Cape Gloucester, one mass of active craters, with several smaller craters along the coast line from Cape Wilson to Cape Gloucester. Ninth, Tupinier Island—active. Tenth, Rook Island—extinct. Thus making a total of ten actual groups of volcanoes, more or less active, whilst on the south side there is but one, Cape Quoy; and it is very doubtful to me if that has ever been a volcano, but rather an upheaval. I have purposely omitted the Byning Mountains, as there is no distinct crater to be seen amongst them; their very rugged appearance would lead me to imagine that they also were the result of some mighty convulsion when the earth was in the throes of conception. It is a fact worthy of note that there is no appearance of volcanoes, active or extinct, on New Ireland.

(26.) Before closing these necessarily slight notes of these most interesting islands I should like to express my earnest hope that the day is not far distant when an expedition will be fitted out to visit them. I do not mean an Admiralty expedition; for, although there are no men on the face of the earth better able to carry one out than our gallant naval officers, there are many reasons why such an expedition as the one I hope to see should be comparatively a private one. The very mention of a man-of-war in sight is enough to send the natives of some places off to hide in the bush. The vessel I should propose would be a small one—say one hundred tons—and built of wood, with an auxiliary steam power, which is invaluable on approaching a dangerous island or harbour, and also in calms. She should have a small complement of steady men and officers, with one to command who has considerable knowledge of natives, with the necessary scientific collectors; and should be stored for two years. The smallness of the vessel, with her auxiliary screw, would enable her to enter every little hole and corner on a coast, making complete anthropological, botanical, and zoological collections. The commander should at all times be prepared to visit the chiefs, and if necessary stay with them two or three days, to enable the collectors to make a satisfactory collection, at the same time acquiring what information he could as to the habits and customs of the natives, as well as an exact account of the uses they make of their various ornaments, implements and weapons, &c. A slight outline survey of places called at should also be made, and where practicable dredging should be carried on ; but it would also be necessary to the success of the undertaking that all scientists, as well as others, should be under the complete control of the commander. The vessel should be fitted with everything necessary for carrying out all the objects of the expedition, and her furnaces should be so constructed that she could burn wood when under steam.

Valuable time is being wasted ; every year sees these natives in a less primitive condition than the former one ; indeed in some places races are dying out before the advance of civilisation, as is the case in some of the Line Islands. The trade carried on with these islands is itself a terrible destroyer of their primævalism, supplying goods from Europe that superseded their ancient and original manufactures, and cause them in a few years to die out and be lost. Instead of the stone tomahawk is used the iron one, the musket instead of the spear, bow and arrow, or sling, cloth for tapa, beads for shells, and even the ancient head-dress has in some instances given way to hats or bonnets. Thus the destruction of original peculiarities is generally on the increase, spreading as the trade increases, and will no doubt at some future date as irrevocably destroy the ancient style and habits of these as it has of other nations ; nor will this be at so distant a period as some might think, for an island is not like a continent, but is smaller, and the natives sooner succumb to the insidious trader. Therefore if a record of these people in their

original state is to be handed down to posterity no further
time should be lost; what has been thrown away c n never
be regained, but it is possible to prevent further loss of time
by immediate action, and it is my earnest and sincere hope
that these suggestions may be acted on, and that those
interested in the aborignal races of the Pacific may not
have to mourn the impossibility of obtaining such records
and information by putting off doing so till too late.

VOCABULARY OF WORDS.

(*From the Italian.*)

English.	Duke of York. (Mowlett.)	New Britain. (Kininigunun.)	New Ireland. (Karlisle.
Armlet	..	a lili	
Axe	a pem	a pem	
Bamboo	a kauri	a kauri	
Banana	a wudu	a wudu	
Basket	a rat	a rat	
Barter (v.)	..	lugara	
Beads	a vinadĕwai	a piova	
Beetle	..	a kua-ri	
Betel-nut	a boa	a bue	
Bird	a pika	a beyo	
Boy	a nat	..	
Bush (inland)	..	a rapapupai	
Butterfly	a tortô	a bebi	
Cane	a kĕdda	a kĕdda	
Canoe (large) (without outrigger)	a mworn	a mworn	mworn
Canoe (small) (with outrigger)	o-aga	o-aga	
Caterpillar	a auvi	a olĩva	
Crocodile	a pŭk pŭk	a pŭk pŭk	
Chrysalis	..	a babinum	
Cloth (native)	a mãlu	a mãlu	
Club (stone)	..	a ramnat	
Club (wood)	..	a ram	
Cocoa-nut (young)	a terrip	a terrip	a terris
Cocoa-nut (older)	a kulau	a kulau	a kulas
Cocoa-nut (not quite ripe)	a kubika	a kubika	a kubis
Cocoa-nut (old)	a alamai	a alamai	a alamas
Dance	a mulãgin	a mulãgin	
Dead	mat	mat	
Devil	a toberan	a toberan	
Dog (as in *cut*)	a pup	a pup	pupa
Earring	..	a maritalãghina	
Egg	a kiau	a kiau	

English.	Duke of York. (Mowlett.)	New Britain. (Kininigunun.)	New Ireland. (Karlisle.)
Feather head-dress	a lukwar	a lukwar	
Fire (as in *cut*)	ungwin	ai-ăp	ai-ă
Fish (Eng. *ine*)	ain	a ain	
Fishing-net	aubanang	aubĭn	
Fishing-basket (or trap) (Eng. *woop*)	..	a ŭp	
Fool	a long-long	a long-long	
Fowl	a kărăki	a kakaruka	
Frog	a rok-rok	a rok-rok	
Give me (v.)	..	a nakabea	
Girl	..	a garravafini	
Grass (long)	a kunai	a kunai	
Haul (to pull) (v.)	alla	..	
House	a ruma	a păl	
Husk (outside of old cocoa-nut)	a palalamai	a palalamai	a palalamas
Husk (outside of young cocoa-nut)	a palakulau	a palakulau	a palakulus
Jew's Harp	..	a ungap	
Knife	a burnam	a burnam	
Leaf	a ghilai	a bui / a mapinai	
Let go (v.)	palai	..	
Look out (to look at that)	..	terua / boi-boi	
Man	a mwoana / a tira	a tutuana	
Money	diwarra	a tabu	
Make haste	a alŭt	ai-ap	
Necklace	..	kurakurŭa	
Necklace (of beads)	..	unghid	
No	puta	pută	
Nose stick (horizontal)	..	a bilibăgo	
Nose stick (through nostril)	..	ai bŭta	
Paint (red earth)	..	a tara	
Paint (blue earth)	..	a pepen	
Pearl shell	a kălăng	a kalăgi	
Pig	boroi	boroi	boroi
Pigeon	kurŭa	balu	
Pipe (tobacco)	..	piet-moa	
Rain	a băta	a băta	
Rat	a gălăng	a gălăng	
Reef (or big stone)	awăt (or avăt)	awăto (or avăto)	
Rope	we we	raoa	
Salt	..	a ta	
Sand	ă ragai	..	
Shell (sea)	..	a vinaganoi	
Shell (land)	..	a kato	
Ship	a prao	a prao	

English.	New Britain. (Kininigunun.)	Duke of York. (Mowlett.)	New Ireland. (Karlisle.)
Shore	a rualine	a rualine	
Sick	mulapang	mati	
Skeleton	..	lala-laluna	
Skull (or head)	a lorigne	a luna	
Sling	..	waiwi	
Snake	a ôbi (or ôrbi)	a ôvi (or ôvri)	
Song	a kele-kele	a kele-kele	
Spear	a bele	a ruma	
Stone axe	..	barur	
Stone (small)	..	a ruru	
Sweet potato	a mămi	a mămi	
Taro	a pâ	a pâ	
Tobacco	..	a sukr	
Turtle	a pŭn	a pŭn	a pŭn
Turtle shell	pelapŭn	pelapŭn	pelapŭn
Wallaby	a aukin	a aukin	
Water (fresh)	a danim	a ta va	
Water (salt)	a tă	a tai	
White (or lime)	a kabang	a kabang	
Wind (N. W. monsoon)	a tobarr	a tobarr	a tobarr
Wind (S.E. monsoon)	a labĕru	a labĕru	a labĕru
Woman	a vafini	a tabuan	
Wood or tree	a dewai	a dewai	
Yam	a ôp	a ôp	
Yes	er	er	

NUMBERS.

GAZELLE PENINSULA, NEW BRITAIN.

1. Tikai.
2. Urua.
3. O Tul.
4. Ivăt.
5. A-lima.
6. Lip tikai.
7. Lov-urua.
8. Lov-otul.
9. Lov-ivăt.
10. Turàlim (or tu-à-lim).
10. (together) Ave-nun.
20. {   „   Ur-ave-nun.
    „   Urua tanivat (alim).
30.   „   Ot-ave-nun.
100.   „   Amăra.

LONDON :
PRINTED BY WILLIAM CLOWES AND SONS, LIMITED,
STAMFORD STREET AND CHARING CROSS.